Spiritual Strength for Men
ߐ

Spiritual Strength for Men

Selections from the Writings
of Bahá'u'lláh, the Báb, and 'Abdu'l-Bahá

Kalimát Press • Los Angeles

Copyright © 2002 by Kalimát Press
Second printing 2003
All Rights Reserved
Manufactured in Canada

Library of Congress Cataloging-in-Publication Data

Bahá'u'lláh, 1817-1892.
Spiritual strength for men : selections from the writings
of Bahá'u'lláh, the Bab, and 'Abdu'l-Bahá.
p. cm.
ISBN 1-890688-28-2
1. Bahai men--Prayer-books and devotions--English.
2. Bahai Faith--Prayer-books and devotions--English.
I. Bab, 'Ali Muhammad Shirazi, 1819-1850.
II. 'Abdu'l-Bahá, 1844-1921. III. Title.
BP360 .B34 2002
297.9'382--dc21   2002028791

Kalimát Press
1600 Sawtelle Boulevard
Suite 310
Los Angeles, California 90025

www.kalimat.com
kalimatp@aol.com

CONTENTS

§§

The headings designated below are purely arbitrary, for the purpose of easier location of the prayers. They form no part of the Sacred Text itself.

Instructions

A New Race of Men   3
Army of God   9
Instructions   18
Gird Up Thy Loins   24

Prayers and Passages

Assistance   33
Courage   38
Debts   42
Firmness   46
Forgiveness   48
Gratitude   55
Healing   63
Independence   67
Leadership   70
Marriage   75

Parents 82
Praise 86
Sacrifice 92
Service 97
Sons and Daughters 102
Strength 110
Success 115
True Wealth 118
Work 123

Tablets and Meditations

Tablet of Aḥmad 131
Tablet on Purity 136
Tablet of the Hair 146
The Maid of Heaven 151
Tablet of the Virgin 157

MY NAME IS 'ABDU'L-BAHÁ*
My qualification is 'Abdu'l-Bahá.
My reality is 'Abdu'l-Bahá.
My praise is 'Abdu'l-Bahá.
Thraldom to the Blessed Perfection
  is my glorious and refulgent diadem, and
  servitude to all the human race
  my perpetual religion . . .
No name,
no title,
no mention,
no commendation have I,
  nor will ever have,
  except 'Abdu'l-Bahá.
This is my longing.
This is my greatest yearning.
This is my eternal life.
This is my everlasting glory.

—'Abdu'l-Bahá

§§

*Literally, Servant of Glory.

'ABDU'L-BAHÁ AS A YOUNG MAN

INSTRUCTIONS

*That one indeed is a man
who, today, dedicateth himself
to the service
of the entire human race.
The Great Being saith:
Blessed and happy is he
that ariseth to promote
the best interests
of the peoples and kindreds of the earth.*
—Bahá'u'lláh

A New Race of Men

> . . . *the supreme and distinguishing function of His Revelation . . . is none other than the calling into being of a new race of men . . .*
> —Shoghi Effendi

A RACE OF MEN, incomparable in character, shall be raised up which, with the feet of detachment, will tread under all who are in heaven and on earth, and will cast the sleeve of holiness over all that hath been created from water and clay.

—Bahá'u'lláh

§§

IS NOT THE OBJECT of every Revelation to effect a transformation in the whole character of mankind, a transformation that shall manifest itself both outwardly and inwardly, that shall affect both its inner life and external conditions? For if the character of mankind be not changed, the futility of God's universal Manifestation would be apparent.

—*Bahá'u'lláh*

§§

THERE LAY concealed within the Holy Veil, and prepared for the service of God, a company of His chosen ones who shall be manifested unto men, who shall aid His Cause, who shall be afraid of no one, though the entire human race rise up and war against them. These are the ones who, before the gaze of the dwellers on earth and the denizens of heaven, shall arise and, shouting aloud, acclaim the name of the Almighty, and summon the children of men to the path of God, the All-Glorious, the All-Praised.

Walk thou in their way, and let no one dismay thee. Be of them whom the tumult of the world, however much it may agitate them in the path of their Creator, can never sadden, whose purpose the blame of the blamer will never defeat.

Go forth with the Tablet of God and His signs, and rejoin them that have believed in Me, and announce unto them tidings of Our most holy Paradise.

—*Bahá'u'lláh*

§§

BAHÁ'U'LLÁH—may my life, my soul, my spirit be offered up as a sacrifice unto His lowly servants—hath, during His last days on earth, given the most emphatic promise that, through the outpourings of the grace of God and the aid and assistance vouchsafed from His

Kingdom on high, souls will arise and holy beings appear who, as stars, would adorn the firmament of divine guidance; illumine the dayspring of loving-kindness and bounty; manifest the signs of the unity of God; shine with the light of sanctity and purity; receive their full measure of divine inspiration; raise high the sacred torch of faith; stand firm as the rock and immoveable as the mountain; and grow to become luminaries in the heavens of His Revelation, mighty channels of His grace, means for the bestowal of God's bountiful care, heralds calling forth the name of the One true God, and establishers of the world's supreme foundation.

These shall labor ceaselessly, by day and by night, shall heed neither trials nor woe, shall suffer no respite in their efforts, shall seek no repose, shall disregard all ease and comfort, and, detached and unsullied, shall consecrate every fleeting moment of their lives to the diffusion of the divine fragrance and the exaltation of God's holy Word. Their faces will radiate heavenly gladness, and their hearts be filled with joy. Their souls will be inspired, and their foundation stand secure. They shall scatter in the world, and travel throughout all regions. They shall raise their voices in every assembly, and adorn and revive every gathering. They shall speak in every tongue, and interpret every hidden meaning. They shall reveal the mysteries of the Kingdom, and manifest unto everyone the signs of God. They shall burn brightly even as a candle in the heart of every assembly, and beam forth as a star upon every horizon. The gentle breezes wafted from the garden of their hearts shall perfume and revive the souls of men, and the revelations of their minds, even as showers, will reinvigorate the peoples and nations of the world.

I am waiting, eagerly waiting for these holy ones to appear; and yet, how long will they delay their coming? My prayer and ardent supplication, at eventide and at dawn, is that these shining stars may soon shed their radiance upon the world, that their sacred countenances may be unveiled to mortal eyes, that the hosts of divine assistance may achieve their victory, and the billows of grace, rising from His oceans above, may flow upon all mankind. Pray ye also and supplicate unto Him that through the bountiful aid of the Ancient Beauty these souls may be unveiled to the eyes of the world.

—'Abdu'l-Bahá

Army of God

When soldiers of the world draw their swords to kill, soldiers of God clasp each other's hands! So may all the savagery of man disappear by the Mercy of God, working through the pure in heart and the sincere of soul.
—'Abdu'l-Bahá

O THOU INCOMPARABLE GOD! O Thou Lord of the Kingdom! These souls are Thy heavenly army. Assist them and, with the cohorts of the Supreme Concourse, make them victorious, so that each one of them may become like unto a regiment and conquer these countries through the love of God and the illumination of divine teachings.

O God! Be Thou their supporter and their

helper, and in the wilderness, the mountain, the valley, the forests, the prairies and the seas, be Thou their confidant—so that they may cry out through the power of the Kingdom and the breath of the Holy Spirit.

Verily, Thou art the Powerful, the Mighty and the Omnipotent, and Thou art the Wise, the Hearing and the Seeing.

—'Abdu'l-Bahá

§§

O ARMY OF GOD! Today, in this world, every people is wandering astray in its own desert, moving here and there according to the dictates of its fancies and whims, pursuing its own particular caprice. Amongst all the teeming masses of the earth, only this community of the Most Great Name is free and clear of human schemes and hath no selfish purpose to promote. Alone amongst them all, this people hath arisen with aims purified of self, following the Teachings of God, most eagerly toiling and striving toward a single goal: to turn this nether dust into high heaven, to make of this world a mirror for the Kingdom, to change this world into a different world, and cause all humankind to adopt the ways of righteousness and a new manner of life.

O army of God!

Through the protection and help vouchsafed by the Blessed Beauty—may my life be a sacrifice to His loved ones—ye must conduct yourselves in such a manner that ye may stand out distinguished and brilliant as the sun among other souls. Should any one of you enter a city, he should become a center of attraction by reason of his sincerity, his faithfulness and love, his honesty and fidelity, his truthfulness and loving-kindness towards all the peoples of the world, so that the people of that city may cry out and say: "This man is unquestionably a Bahá'í, for his manners, his behavior, his conduct, his morals, his nature, and disposition reflect the attributes of the Bahá'ís." Not until ye attain this station can ye be said to have been faithful to the Covenant and Testament of God. For He hath, through irrefutable Texts, entered into a binding Covenant with us all, requiring us to act in accordance with His sacred instructions and counsels.

O army of God!

The time hath come for the effects and perfections of the Most Great Name to be made manifest in this excellent age, so as to establish, beyond any doubt, that this era is the era of Bahá'u'lláh, and this age is distinguished above all other ages.

O army of God!

Whensoever ye behold a person whose entire attention is directed toward the Cause of God; whose only aim is this, to make the Word of God to take effect; who, day and night, with pure intent, is rendering service to the Cause; from whose behavior not the slightest trace of egotism or private motives is discerned—who, rather, wandereth distracted in the wilderness of the love of God, and drinketh only from the cup of the knowledge of God, and is utterly engrossed in spreading the sweet savors of God, and is enamored of the holy verses of the Kingdom of God—know ye for a certainty that this individual will be supported and reinforced by heaven; that like unto the morning star, he will forever gleam brightly out of the skies of eternal grace. But if he show the slightest taint of selfish desires and self-love, his efforts will lead to nothing and he will be destroyed and left hopeless at the last.

O army of God!

Praise be to God, Bahá'u'lláh hath lifted the chains from off the necks of humankind, and hath set man free from all that trammeled him, and told him: Ye are the fruits of one tree and the leaves of one branch; be ye compassionate and kind to all the human race. Deal ye with strangers the same as with friends, cherish ye others just as ye would your own. See foes as friends; see demons as angels; give to the tyrant the same great love ye show the loyal and true, and even as gazelles from the scented cities of

Khatá and Khutan* offer up sweet musk to the ravening wolf. Be ye a refuge to the fearful; bring ye rest and peace to the disturbed; make ye a provision for the destitute; be a treasury of riches for the poor; be a healing medicine for those who suffer pain; be ye doctor and nurse to the ailing; promote ye friendship, and honor, and conciliation, and devotion to God, in this world of non-existence.

O army of God!

Make ye a mighty effort: perchance ye can flood this earth with light, that this mud hut, the world, may become the Abhá Paradise. The dark hath taken over, and the brute traits prevail. This world of man is now an arena for wild beasts, a field where the ignorant, the heedless, seize their chance. The souls of men are ravening wolves and animals with blinded eyes, they are either deadly poison or useless weeds—all except for a very few who indeed do nurture altruistic aims and plans for the well-being of

---

*Cities in China celebrated for their musk perfumes.

their fellow men: but ye must in this matter—that is, the serving of humankind—lay down your very lives, and as ye yield yourselves, rejoice.

O army of God!

The Exalted One, the Báb, gave up His life. The Blessed Perfection gave up a hundred lives at every breath. He bore calamities. He suffered anguish. He was imprisoned. He was chained. He was made homeless and was banished to distant lands. Finally, then, He lived out His days in the Most Great Prison. Likewise, a great multitude of the lovers of God who followed this path have tasted the honey of martyrdom and they gave up everything—life, possessions, kindred—all they had. How many homes were reduced to rubble; how many dwellings were broken into and pillaged; how many a noble building went to the ground; how many a palace was battered into a tomb. And all this came about that humankind might be illumined, that ignorance might yield to knowledge, that men of earth might become men of heaven, that discord and dissension might be torn out by the roots, and the Kingdom of Peace become established over all the world. Strive ye now that this bounty become manifest, and this best-beloved of all hopes be realized in splendor throughout the community of man.

O army of God!

Beware lest ye harm any soul, or make any heart to sorrow; lest ye wound any man with your words, be he known to you or a stranger, be he friend or foe. Pray ye for all; ask ye that all be blessed, all be forgiven. Beware, beware, lest any of you seek vengeance, even against one who is thirsting for your blood. Beware, beware, lest ye offend the feelings of another, even though he be an evil-doer, and he wish you ill. Look ye not upon the creatures, turn ye to their Creator. See ye not the never-yielding people, see but the Lord of Hosts. Gaze ye not down upon the dust, gaze upward at the shining sun, which hath caused every patch of darksome earth to glow with light.

O army of God!

When calamity striketh, be ye patient and composed. However afflictive your sufferings may be, stay ye undisturbed, and with perfect confidence in the abounding grace of God, brave ye the tempest of tribulations and fiery ordeals.

—'Abdu'l-Bahá

INSTRUCTIONS

It is your duty to be exceedingly kind to every human being, and to wish him well; to work for the upliftment of society; to blow the breath of life into the dead; to act in accordance with the instructions of Bahá'u'lláh and walk His path—until ye change the world of man into the world of God.
—'Abdu'l-Bahá

BE GENEROUS IN PROSPERITY, and thankful in adversity. Be worthy of the trust of thy neighbor, and look upon him with a bright and friendly face. Be a treasure to the poor, an admonisher to the rich, an answerer of the cry of the needy, a preserver of the sanctity of thy pledge. Be fair in thy judgment, and guarded in thy speech. Be unjust to no man, and show all meekness to all men. Be as a lamp unto them that walk in darkness, a joy to the sorrowful, a sea for the thirsty, a haven for the distressed, an upholder and defender of the victim of oppression.

Let integrity and uprightness distinguish all thine acts. Be a home for the stranger, a balm to the suffering, a tower of strength for the fugitive. Be eyes to the blind, and a guiding light unto the feet of the erring.

Be an ornament to the countenance of truth, a crown to the brow of fidelity, a pillar of the temple of righteousness, a breath of life to the body of mankind, an ensign of the hosts of justice, a luminary above the horizon of virtue, a dew to the soil of the human heart, an ark on the ocean of knowledge, a sun in the heaven of bounty, a gem on the diadem of wisdom, a shining light in the firmament of thy generation, a fruit upon the tree of humility.

—Bahá'u'lláh

To LIVE THE LIFE IS: To be no cause of grief to anyone.

To be kind to all people and to love them with a pure spirit.

Should opposition or injury happen to us, to bear it, to be as kind as ever we can be, and through all, to love the people. Should calamity exist in the greatest degree, to rejoice, for these things are the gifts and favors of God.

To be silent concerning the faults of others, to pray for them; and to help them, through kindness, to correct their faults.

To look always at the good and not at the bad. If a man has ten good qualities and one bad one, look at the ten and forget the one. And if a man has ten bad qualities and one good one, to look at the one and forget the ten.

Never to allow ourselves to speak one unkind word about another, even though that other be our enemy.

To do all our deeds in kindness.

To sever our hearts from ourselves and from the world.

To be humble.

To be servants of each other, and to know that we are less than anyone else.

To be as one soul in many bodies; for the more we love each other, the nearer we shall be to God; but to know that our love, our unity, our obedience must not be by confession, but of reality.

To act with cautiousness and wisdom.

To be truthful.

To be hospitable.

To be reverent.

To be a cause of healing for every sick one, a comforter of every sorrowing one, a pleasant water for every thirsty one, a heavenly table for every hungry one, a star to every horizon, a light for every lamp, a herald to everyone who yearns for the kingdom of God.

—'Abdu'l-Bahá

§§

O FRIENDS OF GOD! If ye will trust in the Word of God and be strong; if ye will follow the precepts of Bahá'u'lláh to tend the sick, raise the fallen, care for the poor and needy, give shelter to the destitute, protect the oppressed, comfort the sorrowful and love the world of humanity with all your hearts, then I say unto you that ere long this meeting-place will see a wonderful harvest. Day by day each member will advance and become more and more spiritual.

But ye must have a firm foundation and your aims and ambitions must be clearly understood by each member. They shall be as follows:

1. To show compassion and goodwill to all mankind.

2. To render service to humanity.

3. To endeavor to guide and enlighten those in darkness.

4. To be kind to everyone, and show forth affection to every living soul.

5. To be humble in your attitude towards God, to be constant in prayer to Him, so as to grow daily nearer to God.

6. To be so faithful and sincere in all your actions that every member may be known as embodying the qualities of honesty, love, faith, kindness, generosity, and courage. To be detached from all that is not God, attracted by the Heavenly Breath—a divine soul; so that the world may know that a Baha'i is a perfect being. Strive to attain this at these meetings. Then, indeed and in truth will ye, the friends of God, come together with great joy! Render help one to the other, become as one man, having reached perfect unity.

I pray to God that daily ye may advance in spirituality, that God's love may be more and more manifested in you, that the thoughts of your hearts may be purified, and that your faces may be ever turned towards Him. May you one and all approach to the threshold of unity, and enter into the Kingdom. May each of you be like unto a flaming torch, lighted and burning bright with the fire of the Love of God.

— 'Abdu'l-Bahá

GIRD UP THY LOINS

Happy art thou to have girded thy loins in service . . .
—*'Abdu'l-Bahá*

GIRD UP THE LOINS of thine endeavor, that haply thou mayest guide thy neighbor to the law of God, the Most Merciful. Such an act, verily, excelleth all other acts in the sight of God, the All-Possessing, the Most High. Such must be thy steadfastness in the Cause of God, that no earthly thing whatsoever will have the power to deter thee from thy duty. Though the powers of earth be leagued against thee, though all men dispute with thee, thou must remain unshaken.

—*Bahá'u'lláh*

§§

GIRD UP THE LOINS of your endeavor, O people of Bahá, that haply the tumult of religious dissension and strife that agitateth the peoples of the earth may be stilled, that every trace of it may be completely obliterated. For the love of God, and them that serve Him, arise to aid this sublime and momentous Revelation. . . .

The utterance of God is a lamp, whose light is these words: Ye are the fruits of one tree, and the leaves of one branch. Deal ye one with another with the utmost love and harmony, with friendliness and fellowship. He Who is the Daystar of Truth beareth Me witness! So powerful is the light of unity that it can illuminate the whole earth. The One true God, He Who knoweth all things, Himself testifieth to the truth of these words.

—*Bahá'u'lláh*

§§

Arise for the triumph of My Cause, and, through the power of thine utterance, subdue the hearts of men. Thou must show forth that which will ensure the peace and the well-being of the miserable and the down-trodden.

Gird up the loins of thine endeavor, that perchance thou mayest release the captive from his chains, and enable him to attain unto true liberty. Justice is, in this day, bewailing its plight, and Equity groaneth beneath the yoke of oppression. The thick clouds of tyranny have darkened the face of the earth, and enveloped its peoples.

Through the movement of Our Pen of glory We have, at the bidding of the omnipotent Ordainer, breathed a new life into every human frame, and instilled into every word a fresh potency. All created things proclaim the evidences of this worldwide regeneration. This is the most great, the most joyful tidings imparted by the Pen of this wronged One to mankind.

Wherefore fear ye, O My well-beloved ones? Who is it that can dismay you? A touch of moisture sufficeth to dissolve the hardened clay out of which this perverse generation is molded. The mere act of your gathering together is enough to scatter the forces of these vain and worthless people.

—Bahá'u'lláh

§§

Now is the time to serve, now is the time to be on fire. Know ye the value of this chance, this favorable juncture that is limitless grace, ere it slip from your hands.

Soon will our handful of days, our vanishing life, be gone, and we shall pass, empty-handed, into the hollow that is dug for those who speak no more; wherefore must we bind our hearts to the manifest Beauty, and cling to the lifeline that faileth never.

We must gird ourselves for service, kindle love's flame, and burn away in its heat. We must loose our tongues till we set the wide world's heart afire, and with bright rays of guidance blot out the armies of the night, and then, for His sake, on the field of sacrifice, fling down our lives.

—*'Abdu'l-Bahá*

Prayers and Passages

*Be thou of the people of hell-fire,
but be not a hypocrite.*

*Be thou an unbeliever,
but be not a plotter.*

*Make thy home in taverns,
but tread not the path of the mischief-maker.*

*Fear thou God,
but not the priest.*

*Give to the executioner thy head,
but not thy heart.*

*Let thine abode be under the stone,
but seek not the shelter of the cleric.*

Thus doth the Holy Reed intone its melodies, and the Nightingale of Paradise warble its song, so that He may infuse life eternal into the mortal frames of men, impart to the temples of dust the essence of the Holy Spirit and the heavenly Light, and draw the transient world, through the potency of a single word, unto the Everlasting Kingdom.

—Bahá'u'lláh

Assistance

God grant that through His gracious and invisible assistance, thou mayest divest thy body and soul of the old garment, and array thyself with the new and imperishable attire.

—Bahá'u'lláh

O GOD, MY GOD! I bear witness to Thy unity and Thy oneness, and that Thou art God, and that there is none other God but Thee. Thou hast everlastingly been sanctified above the mention of any one but Thee and the praise of all else except Thyself, and Thou wilt everlastingly continue to be the same as Thou wast from the beginning and hast ever been. I beseech Thee, O King of Eternity, by the Most

Great Name, and by the effulgences of the Daystar of Thy Revelation upon the Sinai of Utterance, and by the billows of the Ocean of Thy knowledge among all created things, to graciously assist Me in that which will draw Me nigh unto Thee, and will detach Me from all except Thee.

By Thy glory, O Lord of all being, and the Desire of all creation! I would love to lay My face upon every single spot of Thine earth, that perchance it might be honored by touching a spot ennobled by the footsteps of Thy loved ones!

—*Bahá'u'lláh*

§§

FADED NOW is all that erstwhile flourished in the Paradise of Thy transcendent oneness, O my God! Where are the rain-giving clouds of Thy mercy? Shorn are the branches of the Tree of Thy unity of the vesture of Thy majesty and wisdom; where is the springtime of

Thy gifts and bounties? Motionless lies the Ark of Thy Cause on the sea of Thy creation; where are the winds of Thy grace and favors? Encompassed on every side is Thy Lamp by the tempests of discord blowing from every land; where is the globe of Thy graciousness and protection?

Thou seest, O my God, how the eyes of these poor creatures are bent upon the horizon of Thy riches, how the hearts of these helpless ones are set in the direction of Thy might. I beseech Thee, O Thou Who art the sole Desire of them that have recognized Thee, and the Object of the adoration of the entire creation, not to suffer them, now that Thou hast attracted them by Thy most exalted Word, to be far removed from the Tabernacle which Thou hast reared up by Thy name, the All-Glorious.

They are sore pressed with cares, O my Lord, and are encompassed about by the wicked. Send down, therefore, from the heaven of Thy behest Thine invisible hosts, that, holding aloft the ensigns of Thy victory, they may help them in Thy land, and may shield them against Thine adversaries.

—Bahá'u'lláh

§§

My God, my Adored One, my King, my Desire! What tongue can voice my thanks to Thee? I was heedless, Thou didst awaken me. I had turned back from Thee, Thou didst graciously aid me to turn towards Thee. I was as one dead, Thou didst quicken me with the water of life. I was withered, Thou didst revive me with the heavenly stream of Thine utterance which hath flowed forth from the Pen of the All-Merciful.

O Divine Providence! All existence is begotten by Thy bounty; deprive it not of the waters of Thy generosity, neither do Thou withhold it from the ocean of Thy mercy. I beseech Thee to aid and assist me at all times and under all conditions, and seek from the heaven of Thy grace Thine ancient favor. Thou art, in truth, the Lord of bounty, and the Sovereign of the kingdom of eternity.

—*Bahá'u'lláh*

Courage

The source of courage and power is the promotion of the Word of God, and steadfastness in His Love.
—Bahá'u'lláh

Glorified art Thou, O Lord my God! Every man of insight confesseth Thy sovereignty and Thy dominion, and every discerning eye perceiveth the greatness of Thy majesty and the compelling power of Thy might. The winds of tests are powerless to hold back them that enjoy near access to Thee from setting their faces towards the horizon of Thy glory, and the tempests of trials must fail to draw away and hinder such as are wholly devoted to Thy will from approaching Thy court.

Methinks, the lamp of Thy love is burning in their hearts, and the light of Thy tenderness is lit within their breasts. Adversities are incapable of estranging them from Thy Cause, and the vicissitudes of fortune can never cause them to stray from Thy pleasure.

I beseech Thee, O my God, by them and by the sighs which their hearts utter in their separation from Thee, to keep them safe from the mischief of Thine adversaries, and to nourish their souls with what Thou hast ordained for Thy loved ones on whom shall come no fear and who shall not be put to grief.

—*Bahá'u'lláh*

§§

PRAISE BE TO THEE, O Lord, my Best Beloved! Make me steadfast in Thy Cause and grant that I may be reckoned among those who have not violated Thy Covenant nor followed the gods of their own idle fancy. Enable me, then, to obtain a seat of truth in Thy presence, bestow upon me a token of Thy mercy and let me join with such of Thy servants as shall have no fear nor shall they be put to grief.

—*The Báb*

§§

I ASK GOD that His confirmations may encompass you, that your hearts may become radiant, that your eyes become illumined through witnessing the signs of God, that your ears hearken to the anthems of heaven, that your faces be set aglow with the radiant light of the Word of God.

May you all be united, may you be agreed, may you serve the solidarity of mankind. May you be well-wishers of all humanity. May you be assistants of every poor one. May you be nurses for the sick. May you be sources of comfort to the broken in heart. May you be a refuge for the wanderer. May you be a source of courage to the affrighted one.

Thus, through the favor and assistance of God may the standard of the happiness of humanity be held aloft in the center of the world and the ensign of universal agreement be unfurled.

—*'Abdu'l-Bahá*

DEBTS

Whatever evidence of bounty is witnessed in the world, is but an image of His bounty; and every thing owes its existence to His Being . . .
—The Báb

O GOD, and the God of all Names, and Maker of the heavens! I entreat Thee by Thy Name through which He Who is the Day-Spring of Thy might and the Dawning-Place of Thy power hath been manifested, through which every solid thing hath been made to flow, and every dead corpse hath been quickened, and every moving spirit confirmed—I entreat Thee to enable me to rid myself of all attachment to any one but Thee, and to serve Thy Cause, and to wish what Thou didst wish through the power of Thy sovereignty, and to perform what is the good pleasure of Thy will.

I beseech Thee, moreover, O my God, to ordain for me what will make me rich enough to dispense with any one save Thee. Thou seest me, O my God, with my face turned towards Thee, and my hands clinging to the cord of Thy grace. Send down upon me Thy mercy, and write down for me what Thou hast written down for Thy chosen ones. Powerful art Thou to do what pleaseth Thee. No God is there but Thee, the Ever-Forgiving, the All-Bountiful.

—*Bahá'u'lláh*

§§

DISPEL MY GRIEF by Thy bounty and Thy generosity, O God, my God, and banish mine anguish through Thy sovereignty and Thy might. Thou seest me, O my God, with my face set towards Thee at a time when sorrows have compassed me on every side.

I implore Thee, O Thou Who art the Lord of all being, and overshadowest all things visible and invisible, by Thy Name whereby Thou hast subdued the hearts and the souls of men, and by the billows of the Ocean of Thy mercy and the splendors of the Day-Star of Thy bounty, to number me with them whom nothing whatsoever hath deterred from setting their faces toward Thee, O Thou Lord of all names and Maker of the heavens!

Thou beholdest, O my Lord, the things which have befallen me in Thy days. I entreat Thee, by Him Who is the Day-Spring of Thy names and the Dawning-Place of Thine attributes, to ordain for me what will enable me to arise to serve Thee and to extol Thy virtues. Thou art, verily, the Almighty, the Most Powerful, Who art wont to answer the prayers of all men!

And, finally, I beg of Thee by the light of Thy countenance to bless my affairs, and redeem my debts, and satisfy my needs. Thou art He to Whose power and to Whose dominion every tongue hath testified, and Whose majesty and Whose sovereignty every understanding heart hath acknowledged. No God is there but Thee, Who hearest and art ready to answer.

—*Bahá'u'lláh*

Firmness

Rest thou confident that day by day thou shalt progress and wax greater in firmness and in constancy.
—'Abdu'l-Bahá

By God! Though weariness lay me low, and hunger consume me, and the bare rock be my bed, and my fellows the beasts of the field, I will not complain, but will endure patiently as those endued with constancy and firmness have endured patiently, through the power of God, the Eternal King and Creator of the nations, and will render thanks unto God under all conditions.

—*Bahá'u'lláh*

O God, my God! Thou beholdest this weak one begging for celestial strength, this poor one craving Thy heavenly treasures, this thirsty one longing for the fountain of eternal life, this afflicted one yearning for Thy promised healing through Thy boundless mercy which Thou hast destined for Thy chosen servants in Thy kingdom on high.

O Lord! I have no helper save Thee, no shelter besides Thee, and no sustainer except Thee. Assist me with Thine angels to diffuse Thy holy fragrances and to spread abroad Thy teachings amongst the choicest of Thy people.

O my Lord! Suffer me to be detached from aught else save Thee, to hold fast to the hem of Thy bounty, to be wholly devoted to Thy Faith, to remain fast and firm in Thy love and to observe what Thou hast prescribed in Thy Book.

Verily, Thou art the Powerful, the Mighty, the Omnipotent.

—'Abdu'l-Bahá

FORGIVENESS

. . . let repentance be between yourselves and God. He, verily, is the Pardoner, the Bounteous, the Gracious, the One Who absolveth the repentant.
—Bahá'u'lláh

When the sinner findeth himself wholly detached and freed from all save God, he should beg forgiveness and pardon from Him. Confession of sins and transgressions before human beings is not permissible, as it hath never been nor will ever be conducive to divine forgiveness. Moreover such confession before people results in one's humiliation and abasement, and God—exalted be His glory—wisheth not the humiliation of His servants. Verily He is the Compassionate, the Merciful. The sinner should, between himself and God, implore mercy from the Ocean of mercy, beg forgiveness from the Heaven of generosity and say:

O God, my God! I implore Thee by the blood of Thy true lovers who were so enraptured by Thy sweet utterance that they hastened unto the Pinnacle of Glory, the site of the most glorious martyrdom, and I beseech Thee by the mysteries which lie enshrined in Thy knowledge and by the pearls that are treasured in the ocean of Thy bounty to grant forgiveness unto me and unto my father and my mother. Of those who show forth mercy, Thou art in truth the Most Merciful. No God is there but Thee, the Ever-Forgiving, the All-Bountiful.

O Lord! Thou seest this essence of sinfulness turning unto the ocean of Thy favor and this feeble one seeking the kingdom of Thy divine power and this poor creature inclining himself towards the day-star of Thy wealth. By Thy mercy and Thy grace, disappoint him not, O Lord, nor debar him from the revelations of Thy bounty in Thy days, nor cast him away from Thy door which Thou hast opened wide to all that dwell in Thy heaven and on Thine earth.

Alas! Alas! My sins have prevented me from approaching the Court of Thy holiness and my trespasses have caused me to stray far from the Tabernacle of Thy majesty. I have committed that which Thou didst forbid me to do and have put away what Thou didst order me to observe.

I pray Thee by Him Who is the sovereign Lord of Names to write down for me with the Pen of Thy bounty that which will enable me to draw nigh unto Thee and will purge me from my trespasses which have intervened between me and Thy forgiveness and Thy pardon.

Verily, Thou art the Potent, the Bountiful. No God is there but Thee, the Mighty, the Gracious.

—*Bahá'u'lláh*

§§

My God, my God! If none be found to stray from Thy path, how, then, can the ensign of Thy mercy be unfurled, or the banner of Thy bountiful favor be hoisted? And if iniquity be not committed, what is it that can proclaim Thee to be the Concealer of men's sins, the Ever-Forgiving, the Omniscient, the All-Wise? May my soul be a sacrifice to the trespasses of them that trespass against Thee, for upon such trespasses are wafted the sweet savors of the tender mercies of Thy Name, the Compassionate, the All-Merciful. May my life be laid down for the transgressions of such as transgress against Thee, for through them the breath of Thy grace and the fragrance of Thy lovingkindness are made known and diffused amongst men. May my inmost being be offered up for the sins of them that have sinned against Thee, for it is as a result of such sins that the Day Star of Thy manifold favors revealeth itself above the horizon of Thy bounty, and the clouds of Thy never-failing providence rain down their gifts upon the realities of all created things.

I am he, O my Lord, that hath confessed to Thee the multitude of his evil doings, that hath acknowledged what no man hath acknowledged. I have made haste to attain unto the ocean of Thy forgiveness, and have sought shelter beneath the shadow of Thy most gracious favor.

Grant, I beseech Thee, O Thou Who art the Everlasting King and the Sovereign Protector of all men, that I may be enabled to manifest that which shall cause the hearts and souls of men to soar in the limitless immensity of Thy love, and to commune with Thy Spirit. Strengthen me through the power of Thy sovereignty, that I may turn all created things towards the Day Spring of Thy Manifestation and the Source of Thy Revelation.

Aid me, O my Lord, to surrender myself wholly to Thy Will, and to arise and serve Thee, for I cherish this earthly life for no other purpose than to compass the Tabernacle of Thy Revelation and the Seat of Thy Glory. Thou seest me, O my God, detached from all else but Thee, and humble and subservient to Thy Will. Deal with me as it beseemeth Thee, and as it befitteth Thy highness and great glory.

—*Bahá'u'lláh*

§

O Thou kind Lord! We are servants of Thy Threshold, taking shelter at Thy holy Door. We seek no refuge save only this strong pillar, turn nowhere for a haven but unto Thy safekeeping. Protect us, bless us, support us, make us such that we shall love but Thy good pleasure, utter only Thy praise, follow only the pathway of truth, that we may become rich enough to dispense with all save Thee, and receive our gifts from the sea of Thy beneficence, that we may ever strive to exalt Thy Cause and to spread Thy sweet savors far and wide, that we may become oblivious of self and occupied only with Thee, and disown all else and be caught up in Thee.

O Thou Provider, O Thou Forgiver! Grant us Thy grace and loving-kindness, Thy gifts and Thy bestowals, and sustain us, that we may attain our goal. Thou art the Powerful, the Able, the Knower, the Seer; and, verily, Thou art the Generous, and, verily, Thou art the All-Merciful, and, verily, Thou art the Ever-

Forgiving, He to Whom repentance is due, He Who forgiveth even the most grievous of sins.
—*'Abdu'l-Bahá*

GRATITUDE

Were men to discover the motivating purpose of God's Revelation, they would assuredly cast away their fears, and, with hearts filled with gratitude, rejoice with exceeding gladness.
—Bahá'u'lláh

PRAISED BE THOU, Who art the Desire of the world, and thanks be to Thee, O Well-Beloved of the hearts of such as are devoted to Thee!

—*Bahá'u'lláh*

§§

PRAISE BE TO THEE, O my God, that Thou hast revealed Thy favors and Thy boun ties; and glory be to Thee, O my Beloved, that Thou hast manifested the Day-Star of Thy loving-kindness and Thy tender mercies.

I yield Thee such thanks as can direct the steps of the wayward towards the splendors of the morning light of Thy guidance, and enable those who yearn towards Thee to attain the seat of the revelation of the effulgence of Thy beauty.

I yield Thee such thanks as can cause the sick to draw nigh unto the waters of Thy healing, and can help those who are far from Thee to approach the living fountain of Thy presence.

I yield Thee such thanks as can divest the bodies of Thy servants of the garments of mortality and abasement, and attire them in the robes of Thine eternity and Thy glory, and lead the poor unto the shores of Thy holiness and all sufficient riches.

I yield Thee such thanks as can enable the Heavenly Dove to warble forth, upon the branches of the Lote-Tree of Immortality, her song: "Verily, Thou art God. No God is there besides Thee. From eternity Thou hast been exalted above the praise of aught else but Thee, and been high above the description of any one except Thyself."

I yield Thee such thanks as can cause the Nightingale of Glory to pour forth its melody in the highest heaven: " 'Alí,* in truth, is Thy servant, Whom Thou hast singled out from among Thy Messengers and Thy chosen Ones, and made Him to be the Manifestation of Thyself in all that pertaineth unto Thee, and that concerneth the revelation of Thine attributes and the evidences of Thy names."

I yield Thee such thanks as can stir up all things to extol Thee, and to glorify Thine Essence, and can unloose the tongues of all beings to magnify the sovereignty of Thy beauty.

I yield Thee such thanks as can fill the heavens and the earth with the signs of Thy transcendent Essence, and assist all created things to enter the Tabernacle of Thy nearness and Thy presence.

*The Báb.

I yield Thee such thanks as can make every created thing to be a book that shall speak of Thee, and a scroll that shall unfold Thy praise. I yield Thee such thanks as can establish the Manifestations of Thy sovereignty upon the throne of Thy governance, and set up the Exponents of Thy glory upon the seat of Thy Divinity.

I yield Thee such thanks as can make the corrupt tree to bring forth good fruit through the holy breaths of Thy favors, and revive the bodies of all beings with the gentle winds of Thy transcendent grace.

I yield Thee such thanks as can cause the signs of Thine exalted singleness to be sent down out of the heaven of Thy holy unity.

I yield Thee such thanks as can teach all things the realities of Thy knowledge and the essence of Thy wisdom, and will not withhold the wretched creatures from the doors of Thy mercy and Thy bountiful favor.

I yield Thee such thanks as can enable all who are in heaven and on earth to dispense with all created things, through the treasuries of Thine all-sufficing riches, and can aid all created things to reach unto the summit of Thine almighty favors.

I yield Thee such thanks as can assist the hearts of Thine ardent lovers to soar into the atmosphere of nearness to Thee, and of longing for Thee, and kindle the Light of Lights within the land of Iraq.

I yield Thee such thanks as can detach them that are nigh unto Thee from all created things, and draw them to the throne of Thy names and Thine attributes.

I yield Thee such thanks as can cause Thee to forgive all sins and trespasses, and to fulfill the needs of the peoples of all religions, and to waft the fragrances of pardon over the entire creation.

I yield Thee such thanks as can enable them that recognize Thy unity to scale the heights of Thy love, and cause such as are devoted to Thee to ascend unto the Paradise of Thy presence.

I yield Thee such thanks as can satisfy the wants of all such as seek Thee, and realize the aims of them that have recognized Thee.

I yield Thee such thanks as can blot out from the hearts of men all suggestions of limitations, and inscribe the signs of Thy unity.

I yield Thee such thanks as that with which Thou didst from eternity glorify Thine own Self, and didst exalt it above all peers, rivals, and comparisons, O Thou in Whose hands are the heavens of grace and of bounty, and the kingdoms of glory and of majesty!

—*Bahá'u'lláh*

§§

THANKFULNESS is of various kinds. There is a verbal thanksgiving which is confined to a mere utterance of gratitude. This is of no importance because perchance the tongue may give thanks while the heart is unaware of it. Many who offer thanks to God are of this type, their spirits and hearts unconscious of thanksgiving. This is mere usage, just as when we meet, receive a gift and say thank you, speaking the words without significance. One may say *thank you* a thousand times while the heart remains thankless, ungrateful. Therefore, mere verbal thanksgiving is without effect. But real thankfulness is a cordial giving of thanks from the heart. When man in response to the favors of God manifests susceptibilities of conscience, the heart is happy, the spirit is exhilarated. These spiritual susceptibilities are ideal thanksgiving.

There is a cordial thanksgiving, too, which expresses itself in the deeds and actions of man when his heart is filled with gratitude. . . . To express his gratitude for the favors of God man must show forth praiseworthy actions. In response to these bestowals he must render good deeds, be self-sacrificing, loving the servants of God, forfeiting even life for them, showing kindness to all the creatures. He must be severed from the world, attracted to the Kingdom of Abhá, the face radiant, the tongue

eloquent, the ear attentive, striving day and night to attain the good pleasure of God.
—*'Abdu'l-Bahá*

Healing

The remembrance of Thee is a healing medicine to the hearts of such as have drawn nigh unto Thy court . . .
—Bahá'u'lláh

THY NAME IS MY HEALING, O my God, and remembrance of Thee is my remedy. Nearness to Thee is my hope, and love for Thee is my companion. Thy mercy to me is my healing and my succor in both this world and the world to come. Thou, verily, art the All-Bountiful, the All-Knowing, the All-Wise.
—*Bahá'u'lláh*

O God, my God! I beg of Thee by the ocean of Thy healing, and by the splendors of the Daystar of Thy grace, and by Thy Name through which Thou didst subdue Thy servants, and by the pervasive power of Thy most exalted Word and the potency of Thy most august Pen, and by Thy mercy that hath preceded the creation of all who are in heaven and on earth, to purge me with the waters of Thy bounty from every affliction and disorder, and from all weakness and feebleness.

Thou seest, O my Lord, Thy suppliant waiting at the door of Thy bounty, and him who hath set his hopes on Thee clinging to the cord of Thy generosity. Deny him not, I beseech Thee, the things he seeketh from the ocean of Thy grace and the Daystar of Thy loving-kindness.

Powerful art Thou to do what pleaseth Thee. There is none other God save Thee, the Ever-Forgiving, the Most Generous.

—Bahá'u'lláh

§

GLORY BE TO THEE, O Lord my God! I implore Thee by Thy Name, through which Thou didst lift up the ensigns of Thy guidance, and didst shed the radiance of Thy loving-kindness, and didst reveal the sovereignty of Thy Lordship; through which the lamp of Thy names hath appeared within the niche of Thine attributes, and He Who is the Tabernacle of Thy unity and the Manifestation of detachment hath shone forth; through which the ways of Thy guidance were made known, and the paths of Thy good pleasure were marked out; through which the foundations of error have been made to tremble, and the signs of wickedness have been abolished; through which the fountains of wisdom have burst forth, and the heavenly table hath been sent down; through which Thou didst preserve Thy servants and didst vouchsafe Thy healing; through which Thou didst show forth Thy tender mercies unto Thy servants and revealest Thy forgiveness amidst Thy creatures—I implore Thee to keep safe him who hath held fast and returned unto Thee, and clung to Thy mercy, and seized the hem of Thy loving providence. Send down, then, upon him Thy healing, and make him whole, and endue him with a constancy vouchsafed by Thee, and a tranquillity bestowed by Thy highness.

Thou art, verily, the Healer, the Preserver, the Helper, the Almighty, the Powerful, the All-Glorious, the All-Knowing.

—*Bahá'u'lláh*

INDEPENDENCE

All creatures are dependent upon God, however great may seem their knowledge, power and independence.
—'Abdu'l-Bahá

O MY GOD, my Lord and my Master! I have detached myself from my kindred and have sought through Thee to become independent of all that dwell on earth and ever ready to receive that which is praiseworthy in Thy sight. Bestow on me such good as will make me independent of aught else but Thee, and grant me an ampler share of Thy boundless favors. Verily Thou art the Lord of grace abounding.

—*The Báb*

O MY GOD! O Thou Who art the Maker of the heavens and of the earth, O Lord of the Kingdom!

Thou well knowest the secrets of my heart, while Thy Being is inscrutable to all save Thyself. Thou seest whatsoever is of me, while no one else can do this save Thee. Vouchsafe unto me, through Thy grace, what will enable me to dispense with all except Thee, and destine for me that which will make me independent of everyone else besides Thee. Grant that I may reap the benefit of my life in this world and in the next. Open to my face the portals of Thy grace and graciously confer upon me Thy tender mercy and bestowals.

O Thou Who art the Lord of grace abounding! Let Thy celestial aid surround those who love Thee and bestow upon us the gifts and the bounties Thou dost possess. Be Thou sufficient unto us of all things, forgive our sins and have mercy upon us. Thou art Our Lord and the

Lord of all created things. No one else do we invoke but Thee and naught do we beseech but Thy favors. Thou art the Lord of bounty and grace, invincible in Thy power and the most skillful in Thy designs. No God is there but Thee, the All-Possessing, the Most Exalted.

Confer Thy blessings, O my Lord, upon the Messengers, the holy ones and the righteous. Verily Thou art God, the Peerless, the All-Compelling.

—The Báb

LEADERSHIP

Recite thou the verses of guidance. Be engaged in the worship of thy Lord, and rise up to lead the people aright.
—'Abdu'l-Bahá

O YE THE BELOVED of the one true God! Pass beyond the narrow retreats of your evil and corrupt desires, and advance into the vast im-mensity of the realm of God, and abide ye in the meads of sanctity and of detachment, that the fragrance of your deeds may lead the whole of mankind to the ocean of God's unfading glory.

—Bahá'u'lláh

§

Say: Beware, O people of Bahá, lest ye walk in the ways of them whose words differ from their deeds. Strive that ye may be enabled to manifest to the peoples of the earth the signs of God, and to mirror forth His commandments.

Let your acts be a guide unto all mankind, for the professions of most men, be they high or low, differ from their conduct. It is through your deeds that ye can distinguish yourselves from others. Through them the brightness of your light can be shed upon the whole earth.

Happy is the man that heedeth My counsel, and keepeth the precepts prescribed by Him Who is the All-Knowing, the All-Wise.

—*Bahá'u'lláh*

§

O ye who are strongly attracted! O ye who are mindful! O ye who are advancing unto the Kingdom of God! Verily with all my heart and soul and with all lowliness do I supplicate the Lord God to make of you ensigns of guidance, banners of righteousness, well-springs of understanding and knowledge, that through you He may lead the seekers unto the straight path and guide them to the broad way of truth in this mightiest of ages.

—'Abdu'l-Bahá

§§

O MY GOD! O my God! Verily, Thou dost perceive those who are present here turning unto Thee, relying upon Thee. O my Lord! O my Lord! Illumine their eyes by the light of love, and enkindle their hearts by the rays streaming from the heaven of the Supreme Concourse. Suffer them to become the signs of Thy bestowal amongst the people and the standards of Thy grace amongst mankind.

O Lord! Make those who are here the hosts of heaven, and through their service and instrumentality subdue the hearts of humanity. Cause Thy great mercy to descend upon them, and render all Thy friends victorious. Direct them that they may turn toward Thy Kingdom of mercy and proclaim Thy name among the people. May they lead the people to the bounty of Thy most great guidance.

O Lord! O Lord! Cast the glance of Thy mercy upon them all.

O Lord! O Lord! Ordain for them the beauty of Thy holiness in Thy Kingdom of eternity.

O Lord! O Lord! Protect them in every test, make every foot firm in the pathway of Thy love, and help them to be as mighty mountains in Thy Cause so that their faith shall not be wavering, their sight shall not be dimmed nor hindered from witnessing the lights emanating from Thy supreme Kingdom.

Verily, Thou art the Generous. Thou art the Almighty. Verily, Thou art the Clement, the Merciful.

—'Abdu'l-Bahá

O LORD! Make this youth radiant and confer Thy bounty upon this poor creature. Bestow upon him knowledge, grant him added strength at the break of every morn and guard him within the shelter of Thy protection so that he may be freed from error, may devote himself to the service of Thy Cause, may guide the wayward, lead the hapless, free the captives and awaken the heedless, that all may be blessed with Thy remembrance and praise. Thou art the Mighty and the Powerful.

—*'Abdu'l-Bahá*

Marriage

*Among the people of Bahá . . . marriage must be a
union of the body and of the spirit . . .*
—'Abdu'l-Bahá

He is the Bestower, the Bounteous! Praise be to God, the Ancient, the Ever-Abiding, the Changeless, the Eternal! He Who hath testified in His Own Being that verily He is the One, the Single, the Untrammeled, the Exalted. We bear witness that verily there is no God but Him, acknowledging His oneness, confessing His singleness. He hath ever dwelt in unapproachable heights, in the summits of His loftiness, sanctified from the mention of aught save Himself, free from the description of aught but Him.

And when He desired to manifest grace and beneficence to men, and to set the world in order, He revealed observances and created laws; among them He established the law of marriage, made it as a fortress for well-being and salvation, and enjoined it upon us in that which was sent down out of the heaven of sanctity in His Most Holy Book. He saith, great is His glory: "Marry, O people, that from you may appear he who will remember Me amongst My servants; this is one of My commandments unto you; obey it as an assistance to yourselves."

—Bahá'u'lláh

§§

FROM SEPARATION doth every kind of hurt and harm proceed, but the union of created things doth ever yield most laudable results. From the pairing of even the smallest particles in the world of being are the grace and bounty of God made manifest; and the higher the degree, the more momentous is the union. "Glory be to Him Who hath created all the pairs, of such things as earth produceth, and out of men themselves, and of things beyond their ken."*

And above all other unions is that between human beings, especially when it cometh to pass in the love of God. Thus is the primal oneness made to appear; thus is laid the foundation of love in the spirit. It is certain that such a marriage as yours will cause the bestowals of God to be revealed.

—'Abdu'l-Bahá

§§

MARRIAGE, among the mass of the people, is a physical bond, and this union can only be temporary, since it is foredoomed to a physical separation at the close.

Among the people of Bahá, however, mar-

---

*Qur'an 36:36; and cf. 51:49.

riage must be a union of the body and of the spirit as well, for here both husband and wife are aglow with the same wine, both are enamored of the same matchless Face, both live and move through the same spirit, both are illumined by the same glory. This connection between them is a spiritual one, hence it is a bond that will abide forever. Likewise do they enjoy strong and lasting ties in the physical world as well, for if the marriage is based both on the spirit and the body, that union is a true one, hence it will endure. If, however, the bond is physical and nothing more, it is sure to be only temporary, and must inexorably end in separation.

When, therefore, the people of Bahá undertake to marry, the union must be a true relationship, a spiritual coming together as well as a physical one, so that throughout every phase of life, and in all the worlds of God, their union will endure; for this real oneness is a gleaming out of the love of God.

—'Abdu'l-Bahá

§§

HE IS GOD! O peerless Lord! In Thine almighty wisdom Thou hast enjoined marriage upon the peoples, that the generations of men may succeed one another in this contingent world, and that ever, so long as the world shall last, they may busy themselves at the Threshold of Thy oneness with servitude and worship, with salutation, adoration and praise. "I have not created spirits and men, but that they should worship me."* Wherefore, wed Thou in the heaven of Thy mercy these two birds of the nest of Thy love, and make them the means of attracting perpetual grace; that from the union of these two seas of love a wave of tenderness may surge and cast the pearls of pure and goodly issue on the shore of life. "He hath let loose the two seas, that they meet each other: Between them is a barrier which they overpass not. Which then of the bounties of your Lord will ye

---

*Qur'an 51:56.

deny? From each He bringeth up greater and lesser pearls."*

O Thou kind Lord! Make Thou this marriage to bring forth coral and pearls. Thou art verily the All-Powerful, the Most Great, the Ever-Forgiving.

—'Abdu'l-Bahá

§§

PRAISE THOU GOD that in tests thou art firm and steadfast and art holding fast to the Abhá Kingdom. Thou art not shaken by any affliction or disturbed by any calamity. Not until man is tried doth the pure gold distinctly separate from the dross. Torment is the fire of test wherein the pure gold shineth resplendently and the impurity is burned and blackened. At present thou art, praise be to God, firm and steadfast in tests and trials and art not shaken by them.

---

*Qur'an 55:19-22.

Thy wife is not in harmony with thee, but praise be to God, the Blessed Beauty is pleased with thee and is conferring upon thee the utmost bounty and blessings. But still try to be patient with thy wife, perchance she may be transformed and her heart may be illumined.

—'Abdu'l-Bahá

PARENTS

It is seemly that the servant should, after each prayer, supplicate God to bestow mercy and forgiveness upon his parents. Thereupon God's call will be raised: "Thousand upon thousand of what thou hast asked for thy parents shall be thy recompense!"
—The Báb

PRAYER FOR FATHERS

THOU OMNIPOTENT LORD! In this Great Dispensation Thou dost accept the intercession of the sons on behalf of their fathers. This is one of the special infinite Bestowals of this Cycle. Therefore, O Thou kind Almighty! Accept the request of this thy servant at the Threshold of Thy Singleness and submerge his father in the ocean of Thy Grace: Because this son is confirmed in the accomplishment of Thy services and is displaying the utmost of effort at all times in the Pathway of Thy Love!

Verily Thou art the Giver, the Forgiver and the Kind!

—'Abdu'l-Bahá

Other Prayers for Parents

O GOD, MY GOD! I implore Thee by the blood of Thy true lovers who were so enraptured by Thy sweet utterance that they hastened unto the Pinnacle of Glory, the site of the most glorious martyrdom, and I beseech Thee by the mysteries which lie enshrined in Thy knowledge and by the pearls that are treasured in the ocean of Thy bounty to grant forgiveness unto me and unto my father and my mother. Of those who show forth mercy, Thou art in truth the Most Merciful. No God is there but Thee, the Ever-Forgiving, the All-Bountiful.

—Bahá'u'lláh

§§

I BEG THY FORGIVENESS, O my God, and implore pardon after the manner Thou wishest Thy servants to direct themselves to Thee. I beg of Thee to wash away our sins as befitteth Thy Lordship, and to forgive me, my parents, and those who in Thy estimation have entered the abode of Thy love in a manner which is worthy of Thy transcendent sovereignty and well beseemeth the glory of Thy celestial power.

O my God! Thou hast inspired my soul to offer its supplication to Thee, and but for Thee, I would not call upon Thee. Lauded and glorified art Thou; I yield Thee praise inasmuch as Thou didst reveal Thyself unto me, and I beg

Thee to forgive me, since I have fallen short in my duty to know Thee and have failed to walk in the path of Thy love.

—*The Báb*

Praise

That which the people possess, and the treasures of the earth, and that which the rulers and kings own, are not equal in this day to the singing of His praise.
—Bahá'u'lláh

PRAISE BE UNTO THEE, Who art my God and the God of all men, and my Desire and the Desire of all them that have recognized Thee, and my Beloved and the Beloved of such as have acknowledged Thy unity, and the Object of my adoration and of the adoration of them that have near access to Thee, and my Wish and the Wish of such as are wholly devoted to Thee, and my Hope and the Hope of them that have fixed their hearts upon Thee, and my Refuge and the Refuge of all such as have hastened towards Thee, and my Haven and the Haven of whosoever hath repaired unto Thee, and my Goal and the Goal of all them that have set themselves towards Thee, and my Object and the Object of those who have fixed their gaze upon Thee, and my Paradise and the Paradise of them that have ascended towards Thee, and my Lode-star and the Lode-star of all such as yearn after Thee, and my Joy and the Joy of all them that love Thee, and my Light and the Light of all such as have erred and asked to be forgiven by Thee, and my Exultation and the Exultation of all them that remember Thee, and my Stronghold and the Stronghold of all such as have fled to Thee, and my Sanctuary and the Sanctuary of all that dread Thee, and my Lord and the Lord of all such as dwell in the heavens and on the earth!

—Bahá'u'lláh

GLORY BE TO THEE, O my God! The power of Thy might beareth me witness! I can have no doubt that should the holy breaths of Thy loving-kindness and the breeze of Thy bountiful favor cease, for less than the twinkling of an eye, to breathe over all created things, the entire creation would perish, and all that are in heaven and on earth would be reduced to utter nothingness. Magnified, therefore, be the marvelous evidences of Thy transcendent power!

Magnified be the potency of Thine exalted might! Magnified be the majesty of Thine all-encompassing greatness, and the energizing influence of Thy will!

Such is Thy greatness that wert Thou to concentrate the eyes of all men in the eye of one of Thy servants, and to compress all their hearts within his heart, and wert Thou to enable him to behold within himself all the things Thou hast created through Thy power and fashioned through Thy might, and were he to ponder, throughout eternity, over the realms of Thy creation and the range of Thy handiwork, he would unfailingly discover that there is no created thing but is overshadowed by Thine all-conquering power, and is vitalized through Thine all-embracing sovereignty.

Behold me, then, O my God, fallen prostrate upon the dust before Thee, confessing my powerlessness and Thine omnipotence, my poverty and Thy wealth, mine evanescence and Thine eternity, mine utter abasement and Thine infinite glory. I recognize that there is none other God but Thee, that Thou hast no peer nor partner, none to equal or rival Thee. In Thine unapproachable loftiness Thou hast, from eternity, been exalted above the praise of any one but Thee, and shalt continue for ever, in Thy transcendent singleness and glory, to be sanctified from the glorification of any one except Thine own Self.

—*Bahá'u'lláh*

He is the Almighty. Glory be unto Him Who is the Lord of all that are in the heavens and on the earth; He is the All-Wise, the All-Informed.

It is He Who calleth into being whatsoever He willeth at His behest; He is indeed the Clement, the Fashioner.

Say, verily He is equal to His purpose; whomsoever He willeth, He maketh victorious through the power of His hosts; there is none other God but Him, the Mighty, the Wise. His is the kingdom of earth and heaven, and He is the Lord of power and glory.

—*The Báb*

§§

Immeasurably glorified and exalted art Thou. How can I make mention of Thee, O Thou the Beloved of the entire creation; and how can I acknowledge Thy claim, O Thou, before Whom every created thing standeth in awe. The loftiest station to which human perception can soar and the utmost height which the minds and souls of men can scale are but signs created through the potency of Thy command and tokens manifested through the power of Thy Revelation.

Far be it from Thy glory that anyone other than Thee should make mention of Thee or should attempt to voice Thy praise. The very essence of every reality beareth witness to its debarment from the precincts of the court of Thy nearness, and the quintessence of every being testifieth to its failure to attain Thy holy Presence.

Immeasurably glorified and exalted art Thou! That which alone beseemeth Thee is the befitting mention made by Thine Own Self, and that only which is worthy of Thee is the anthem of praise voiced by Thine Own Essence.

—The Báb

SACRIFICE

We were of a truth created for sacrifice, and in this do we take pride before all creation.
—Bahá'u'lláh

I HAVE RENOUNCED my desire for Thy desire, O my God, and my will for the revelation of Thy Will. By Thy glory! I desire neither myself nor my life except for the purpose of serving Thy Cause, and I love not my being save that I may sacrifice it in Thy path.
—*Bahá'u'lláh*

§§

GLORIFIED BE THOU, O my God! Behold Thou my head ready to fall before the sword of Thy Will, my neck prepared to bear the chains of Thy Desire, my heart yearning to be made a target for the darts of Thy Decree, mine eyes expectant to gaze on the tokens and signs of Thy wondrous Mercy. For whatsoever may befall me from Thee is the cherished desire of them who thirst to meet Thee, and the supreme aspiration of such as have drawn nigh unto Thy court.

By the glory of Thy might, O Thou my Well-Beloved! To have sacrificed my life for the Manifestations of Thy Self, to have offered up my soul in the path of the Revealers of Thy wondrous Beauty, is to have sacrificed my spirit for Thy Spirit, my being for Thy Being, my glory for Thy glory. It is as if I had offered up all these things for Thy sake, and for the sake of Thy loved ones.

Though my body be pained by the trials that befall me from Thee, though it be afflicted by the revelations of Thy Decree, yet my soul rejoiceth at having partaken of the waters of Thy Beauty, and at having attained the shores of the ocean of Thine eternity. Doth it beseem a lover to flee from his beloved, or to desert the object of his heart's desire? Nay, we all believe in Thee, and eagerly hope to enter Thy presence.

—*Bahá'u'lláh*

§

O THOU DIVINE PROVIDENCE, pitiful are we, grant us Thy succor; homeless wanderers, give us Thy shelter; scattered, do Thou unite us; astray, gather us to Thy fold; bereft, do Thou bestow upon us a share and portion; athirst, lead us to the well-spring of Life; frail, strengthen us that we may arise to help Thy Cause and offer ourselves as a living sacrifice in the pathway of guidance.

—*'Abdu'l-Bahá*

§

UNTIL A BEING setteth his foot in the plane of sacrifice, he is bereft of every favor and grace; and this plane of sacrifice is the realm of dying to the self, that the radiance of the living God may then shine forth. The martyr's field is the place of detachment from self, that the anthems of eternity may be upraised.

Do all ye can to become wholly weary of self, and bind yourselves to that Countenance of Splendors; and once ye have reached such heights of servitude, ye will find, gathered within your shadow, all created things. This is boundless grace; this is the highest sovereignty; this is the life that dieth not. All else save this is at the last but manifest perdition and great loss.

—'Abdu'l-Bahá

§

O DIVINE PROVIDENCE! Lift to Thy lovers' lips a cup brimful of anguish. To the yearners on Thy pathway, make sweetness but a sting, and poison honey-sweet. Set Thou our heads for ornaments on the points of spears. Make Thou our hearts the targets for pitiless arrows and darts. Raise Thou this withered soul to life on the martyr's field, make Thou his faded heart to drink the draught of tyranny, and thus grow fresh and fair once more. Make him to be drunk with the wine of Thine Eternal Covenant, make him a reveler holding high his cup. Help him to fling away his life; grant that for Thy sake, he be offered up.

Thou art the Mighty, the Powerful. Thou art the Knower, the Seer, the Hearer.

—'Abdu'l-Bahá

SERVICE

That one indeed is a man who, today, dedicateth himself to the service of the entire human race.
—Bahá'u'lláh

GLORY BE TO THEE Who hast caused all the holy Ones to confess their helplessness before the manifold revelations of Thy might, and every Prophet to acknowledge His nothingness at the effulgence of Thine abiding glory. I beseech Thee, by Thy name that hath unlocked the gates of Heaven and filled with ecstasy the Concourse on high, to enable me to serve Thee, in this Day, and to strengthen me to observe that which Thou didst prescribe in Thy Book.

Thou knowest, O my Lord, what is in me; but I know not what is in Thee. Thou art the All-Knowing, the All-Informed.

—*Bahá'u'lláh*

§§

Praised be Thou, O Lord my God! I bear witness that from eternity Thou wert exalted in Thy transcendent majesty and might, and wilt to eternity abide in Thy surpassing power and glory. None in the kingdoms of earth and heaven can frustrate Thy purpose; none throughout the realms of revelation and of creation can prevail against Thee. At Thy command Thou doest what Thou willest, and by the power of Thy sovereignty Thou rulest as Thou pleasest.

I implore Thee, O Thou Who causest the dawn to appear, by Thy Lamp which Thou didst light with the fire of Thy love before all that are in heaven and on earth, and whose flame Thou feedest with the fuel of Thy wisdom in the kingdom of Thy creation, to make me to be of those who have soared in Thine atmosphere, and surrendered their will to Thy decree.

I am all wretchedness, O my Lord, and Thou art the Most Powerful, the Almighty. Have pity upon me by Thy grace and bountiful favor, and graciously aid me to serve Thee and them that are dear to Thee. Potent art Thou to do as Thou willest. No God is there but Thee, the God of strength, of glory and wisdom

—Bahá'u'lláh

§

SERVICE IN LOVE for mankind is unity with God. He who serves has already entered the Kingdom and is seated at the right hand of his Lord.

—'Abdu'l-Bahá

§

Tablet of Visitation for 'Abdu'l-Bahá

Whoso reciteth this prayer with lowliness and fervor will bring gladness and joy to the heart of this Servant; it will be even as meeting Him face to face:

He is the All-Glorious! O God, my God! Lowly and tearful, I raise my suppliant hands to Thee and cover my face in the dust of that Threshold of Thine, exalted above the knowledge of the learned, and the praise of all that glorify Thee. Graciously look upon Thy servant, humble and lowly at Thy door, with the glances of the eye of Thy mercy, and immerse him in the Ocean of Thine eternal grace.

Lord! He is a poor and lowly servant of Thine, enthralled and imploring Thee, captive in Thy hand, praying fervently to Thee, trusting in Thee, in tears before Thy face, calling to Thee and beseeching Thee, saying:

O Lord, my God! Give me Thy grace to serve Thy loved ones, strengthen me in my servitude to Thee, illumine my brow with the light of adoration in Thy court of holiness, and of prayer to Thy Kingdom of grandeur. Help me to be selfless at the heavenly entrance of Thy gate, and aid me to be detached from all things within Thy holy precincts. Lord! Give me to drink from the chalice of selflessness; with its robe clothe me, and in its ocean immerse me. Make me as dust in the pathway of Thy loved ones, and grant that I may offer up my soul for the earth ennobled by the footsteps of Thy chosen ones in Thy path, O Lord of Glory in the Highest.

With this prayer doth Thy servant call Thee, at dawntide and in the night-season. Fulfil his heart's desire, O Lord! Illumine his heart, gladden his bosom, kindle his light, that he may serve Thy Cause and Thy servants.

Thou art the Bestower, the Pitiful, the Most Bountiful, the Gracious, the Merciful, the Compassionate.

—'Abdu'l-Bahá

Sons and Daughters

"Every child is potentially the light of the world..."
—'Abdu'l-Bahá

O THOU PEERLESS LORD! Let this suckling babe be nursed from the breast of Thy loving-kindness, guard it within the cradle of Thy safety and protection and grant that it be reared in the arms of Thy tender affection.

—'Abdu'l-Bahá

ss

O GOD! Rear this little babe in the bosom of Thy love, and give it milk from the breast of Thy Providence. Cultivate this fresh plant in the rose garden of Thy love and aid it to grow through the showers of Thy bounty. Make it a child of the kingdom, and lead it to Thy heavenly realm. Thou art powerful and kind, and Thou art the Bestower, the Generous, the Lord of surpassing bounty.

—'Abdu'l-Bahá

§§

O GOD! Educate these children. These children are the plants of Thine orchard, the flowers of Thy meadow, the roses of Thy garden. Let Thy rain fall upon them; let the Sun of Reality shine upon them with Thy love. Let Thy breeze refresh them in order that they may be trained, grow and develop, and appear in the utmost beauty. Thou art the Giver. Thou art the Compassionate.

—'Abdu'l-Bahá

§§

O Thou kind Lord! These lovely children are the handiwork of the fingers of Thy might and the wondrous signs of Thy greatness. O God! Protect these children, graciously assist them to be educated and enable them to render service to the world of humanity. O God! These children are pearls, cause them to be nurtured within the shell of Thy loving-kindness.

Thou art the Bountiful, the All-Loving.
—'Abdu'l-Bahá

Prayers for Sons

Praised be Thou, O Lord my God! Graciously grant that this infant be fed from the breast of Thy tender mercy and loving providence and be nourished with the fruit of Thy celestial trees. Suffer him not to be committed to the care of anyone save Thee, inasmuch as Thou, Thyself, through the potency of Thy sovereign will and power, didst create and call him into being. There is none other God but Thee, the Almighty, the All-Knowing.

Lauded art Thou, O my Best Beloved, waft over him the sweet savors of Thy transcendent bounty and the fragrances of Thy holy bestowals. Enable him then to seek shelter beneath the shadow of Thy most exalted Name, O Thou Who holdest in Thy grasp the kingdom of names and attributes. Verily, Thou art potent to do what Thou willest, and Thou art indeed the Mighty, the Exalted, the Ever-Forgiving, the Gracious, the Generous, the Merciful.

—*Bahá'u'lláh*

§§

O LORD, MY GOD! This is a child that hath sprung from the loins of one of Thy servants to whom Thou hast granted a distinguished station in the Tablets of Thine irrevocable decree and in the Books of Thy behest.

I beseech Thee by Thy name, whereby everyone is enabled to attain the object of his desire, to grant that this child may become a mature soul amongst Thy servants; cause him to shine forth through the power of Thy name, enable him to utter Thy praise, to set his face towards Thee and to draw nigh unto Thee.

Verily it is Thou Who hast, from everlasting, been powerful to do as Thou willest and Who wilt, to eternity, remain potent to do as Thou pleasest. There is none other God but Thee, the Exalted, the August, the Subduer, the Mighty, the All-Compelling.

—*Bahá'u'lláh*

MEDITATION IN TIMES OF TROUBLE

O PEERLESS LORD! Be Thou a shelter for this poor child and a kind and forgiving Master unto this erring and unhappy soul.

O Lord! Though we are but worthless

plants, yet we belong to Thy garden of roses. Though saplings without leaves and blossoms, yet we are a part of Thine orchard. Nurture this plant then through the outpourings of the clouds of Thy tender mercy and quicken and refresh this sapling through the reviving breath of Thy spiritual springtime.

Suffer him to become heedful, discerning and noble, and grant that he may attain eternal life and abide in Thy Kingdom forevermore.

—'Abdu'l-Bahá

Prayers for Daughters

O THOU MOST GLORIOUS LORD! Make this little maidservant of Thine blessed and happy; cause her to be cherished at the threshold of Thy oneness and let her drink deep from the cup of Thy love so that she may be filled with rapture and ecstasy and diffuse sweet-scented fragrance.

Thou art the Mighty and the Powerful, and Thou art the All-Knowing, the All-Seeing.

—'Abdu'l-Bahá

§§

O Thou kind Lord! Bestow heavenly confirmation upon this daughter of the Kingdom and graciously aid her that she may remain firm and steadfast in Thy Cause and that she may, even as a nightingale of the rose garden of mysteries, warble melodies in the Abhá Kingdom in most wondrous tones, thereby bringing happiness to everyone. Make her exalted among the daughters of the Kingdom and enable her to attain life eternal.

Thou art the Bestower, the All-Loving.

—'Abdu'l-Bahá

§§

O Lord! Help this daughter of the Kingdom to be exalted in both worlds; cause her to turn away from this mortal world of dust and from those who have set their hearts thereon and enable her to have communion and close association with the world of immortality. Give her heavenly power and strengthen her through the breaths of the Holy Spirit that she may arise to serve Thee.

Thou art the Mighty One.

—'Abdu'l-Bahá

STRENGTH

Strengthen the loins of Thy servants in the service of Thy kingdom.
—'Abdu'l-Bahá

O MY LORD! I implore Thee to assist me and them that love me to magnify Thy Word, and to endow us with such strength that the ills of this world and its tribulations will be powerless to hinder us from remembering Thee and from extolling Thy virtues. Powerful art Thou to do all things; resplendent art Thou above all things.

—*Bahá'u'lláh*

§

MY GOD, the Object of my adoration, the Goal of my desire, the All-Bountiful, the Most Compassionate!

All life is of Thee and all power lieth within the grasp of Thine omnipotence. Whosoever Thou exaltest is raised above the angels, and attaineth the station: "Verily, We uplifted him to a place on high!"; and whosoever Thou dost abase is made lower than dust, nay, less than nothing.

O Divine Providence! Though wicked, sinful, and intemperate, we still seek from Thee a "seat of truth," and long to behold the countenance of the Omnipotent King. It is Thine to command, and all sovereignty belongeth to Thee, and the realm of might boweth before Thy behest. Everything Thou doest is pure justice, nay, the very essence of grace. One gleam from the splendors of Thy Name, the All-Merciful, sufficeth to banish and blot out every trace of sinfulness from the world, and a single breath from the breezes of the Day of Thy Revelation is enough to adorn all mankind with a fresh attire.

Vouchsafe Thy strength, O Almighty One, unto Thy weak creatures, and quicken them who are as dead, that haply they may find Thee, and may be led unto the ocean of Thy guidance, and may remain steadfast in Thy Cause. Should the fragrance of Thy praise be shed abroad by any of the divers tongues of the world, out of the East or out of the West, it would, verily, be prized and greatly cherished. If such tongues, however, be deprived of that fragrance, they assuredly would be unworthy of any mention, be they words or thoughts.

We beg of Thee, O Providence, to show Thy way unto all men, and to guide them aright. Thou art, verily, the Almighty, the Most Powerful, the All-Knowing, the All-Seeing.

—*Bahá'u'lláh*

I BESEECH THEE, O my Lord, by Thy most effulgent splendor, before whose brightness every soul humbly boweth down and prostrateth itself in adoration for Thy sake—a splendor before whose radiance fire is turned into light, the dead are brought to life and every difficulty is changed into ease.

I entreat Thee by this great, this wondrous splendor and by the glory of Thine exalted sovereignty, O Thou Who art the Lord of indomitable power, to transform us through Thy bounty into that which Thou Thyself dost possess and enable us to become fountains of Thy light, and graciously vouchsafe unto us that which beseemeth the majesty of Thy transcendent dominion. For unto Thee have I raised my hands, O Lord, and in Thee have I found sheltering support, O Lord, and unto Thee have I resigned myself, O Lord, and upon Thee have I placed my whole reliance, O Lord, and by Thee am I strengthened, O Lord.

Verily there is no power nor strength except in Thee.

—The Báb

O Lord! We are weak; strengthen us. O God! We are ignorant; make us knowing. O Lord! We are poor; make us wealthy. O God! We are dead; quicken us. O Lord! We are humiliation itself; glorify us in Thy Kingdom. If Thou dost assist us, O Lord, we shall become as scintillating stars. If Thou dost not assist us, we shall become lower than the earth.

O Lord! Strengthen us. O God! Confer victory upon us. O God! Enable us to conquer self and overcome desire. O Lord! Deliver us from the bondage of the material world. O Lord! Quicken us through the breath of the Holy Spirit in order that we may arise to serve Thee, engage in worshiping Thee and exert ourselves in Thy Kingdom with the utmost sincerity.

O Lord, Thou art powerful. O God, Thou art forgiving. O Lord, Thou art compassionate.

—'Abdu'l-Bahá

Success

> *The foundation of success and salvation is the knowledge of God . . .*
> —'Abdu'l-Bahá

MAGNIFIED BE THY NAME, O Lord my God! I am the one who hath turned his face towards Thee and hath placed his whole reliance in Thee. I implore Thee by Thy Name whereby the ocean of Thine utterance hath surged and the breezes of Thy knowledge have stirred, to grant that I may be graciously aided to serve Thy Cause and be inspired to remember Thee and praise Thee. Send down then upon me from the heaven of Thy generosity that which will preserve me from anyone but Thee and will profit me in all Thy worlds.

Verily, Thou art the Powerful, the Inaccessible, the Supreme, the Knowing, the Wise.
—Bahá'u'lláh

※

O LORD! Assist those who have renounced all else but Thee, and grant them a mighty victory. Send down upon them, O Lord, the concourse of the angels in heaven and earth and all that is between, to aid Thy servants, to succor and strengthen them, to enable them to achieve success, to sustain them, to invest them with glory, to confer upon them honor and exaltation, to enrich them and to make them triumphant with a wondrous triumph.

Thou art their Lord, the Lord of the heavens and the earth, the Lord of all the worlds. Strengthen this Faith, O Lord, through the power of these servants and cause them to prevail over all the peoples of the world; for they, of a truth, are Thy servants who have detached

themselves from aught else but Thee, and Thou verily art the protector of true believers.
—*The Báb*

§§

DO NOT DESPAIR! Work steadily. Sincerity and love will conquer hate.

How many seemingly impossible events are coming to pass in these days! Set your faces steadily towards the Light of the World. Show love to all; "Love is the breath of the Holy Spirit in the heart of Man."

Take courage! God never forsakes His children who strive and work and pray!

Let your hearts be filled with the strenuous desire that tranquility and harmony may encircle all this warring world. So will success crown your efforts, and with the universal brotherhood will come the Kingdom of God in peace and goodwill.

—*'Abdu'l-Bahá*

True Wealth

By "riches" therefore is meant independence of all else but God, and by "poverty" the lack of things that are of God.
—Bahá'u'lláh

Say: If ye be seekers after this life and the vanities thereof, ye should have sought them while ye were still enclosed in your mothers' wombs, for at that time ye were continually approaching them, could ye but perceive it.

Ye have, on the other hand, ever since ye were born and attained maturity, been all the while receding from the world and drawing closer to dust. Why, then, exhibit such greed in amassing the treasures of the earth, when your days are numbered and your chance is well-nigh lost?

Will ye not, then, O heedless ones, shake off your slumber?

—*Bahá'u'lláh*

§§

LAUDED BE THY NAME, O my God and the God of all things, my Glory and the Glory of all things, my Desire and the Desire of all things, my Strength and the Strength of all things, my King and the King of all things, my Possessor and the Possessor of all things, my Aim and the Aim of all things, my Mover and the Mover of all things! Suffer me not, I implore Thee, to be kept back from the ocean of Thy tender mercies, nor to be far removed from the shores of nearness to Thee.

Aught else except Thee, O my Lord, profiteth me not, and near access to any one save Thyself availeth me nothing. I entreat Thee by the plenteousness of Thy riches, whereby Thou didst dispense with all else except Thyself, to number me with such as have set their faces towards Thee, and arisen to serve Thee.

Forgive, then, O my Lord, Thy servants and Thy handmaidens. Thou, truly, art the Ever-Forgiving, the Most Compassionate.

—Bahá'u'lláh

§§

No MAN OF INSIGHT will let wealth distract his gaze from his ultimate objective, and no man of understanding will allow riches to withhold him from turning unto Him Who is the All-Possessing, the Most High.

Where is he who held dominion over all whereon the sun shineth, who lived extravagantly on earth, seeking out the luxuries of the world and of all that hath been created upon it? . . .

Where are they who went in quest of earthly pleasures and the fruits of carnal desires? Whither are fled their fair and comely women?

Where are their swaying branches, their spreading boughs, their lofty mansions, their trellised gardens? And what of the delights of these gardens—their exquisite grounds and gentle breezes, their purling streams, their soughing winds, their cooing doves and rustling leaves? Where now are their resplendent morns and their brightsome countenances wreathed in smiles?

Alas for them! All have perished and are gone to rest beneath a canopy of dust. Of them one heareth neither name nor mention; none knoweth of their affairs, and naught remaineth of their signs.

What! Will the people dispute then that whereof they themselves stand witness? Will they deny that which they know to be true?

I know not in what wilderness they roam! Do they not see that they are embarked upon a journey from which there is no return? How long will they wander from mountain to valley, from hollow to hill? "Hath not the time come for those who believe to humble their hearts at the mention of God?"*

Blessed is he who hath said, or now shall say, "Yea, by my Lord! The time is come and the hour hath struck!" and who, thereafter, shall detach himself from all that hath been, and deliver himself up entirely unto Him Who is the Possessor of the universe and the Lord of all creation.

—Bahá'u'lláh

---

*Qur'an 57:16.

WORK

The best of men are they that earn a livelihood by their calling and spend upon themselves and upon their kindred for the love of God, the Lord of all worlds.
—Bahá'u'lláh

O PEOPLE OF BAHÁ! It is incumbent upon each one of you to engage in some occupation—such as a craft, a trade or the like. We have exalted your engagement in such work to the rank of worship of the one true God.

Reflect, O people, on the grace and blessings of your Lord, and yield Him thanks at eventide and dawn. Waste not your hours in idleness and sloth, but occupy yourselves with what will profit you and others. Thus hath it been decreed in this Tablet from whose horizon hath shone the day-star of wisdom and utterance.

The most despised of men in the sight of God are they who sit and beg. Hold ye fast unto the cord of means and place your trust in God, the Provider of all means.

—Bahá'u'lláh

§§

O Lord! Unto Thee I repair for refuge, and toward all Thy signs I set my heart.

O Lord! Whether traveling or at home, and in my occupation or in my work, I place my whole trust in Thee. Grant me then Thy sufficing help so as to make me independent of all things, O Thou Who art unsurpassed in Thy mercy!

Bestow upon me my portion, O Lord, as Thou pleasest, and cause me to be satisfied with whatsoever Thou hast ordained for me.

Thine is the absolute authority to command.

—*The Báb*

§§

O THOU SERVANT of the One true God! In this universal dispensation man's wondrous craftsmanship is reckoned as worship of the Resplendent Beauty. Consider what a bounty and blessing it is that craftsmanship is regarded as worship. In former times, it was believed that such skills were tantamount to ignorance, if not a misfortune, hindering man from drawing nigh unto God. Now consider how His infinite bestowals and abundant favors have changed hell-fire into blissful paradise, and a heap of dark dust into a luminous garden.

It behoveth the craftsmen of the world at each moment to offer a thousand tokens of gratitude at the Sacred Threshold, and to exert their highest endeavor and diligently pursue their professions so that their efforts may produce that which will manifest the greatest beauty and perfection before the eyes of all men.

—'Abdu'l-Bahá

§§

I REJOICE TO HEAR that thou takest pains with thine art, for in this wonderful new age, art is worship. The more thou strivest to perfect it, the closer wilt thou come to God. What bestowal could be greater than this: that one's art should be even as the act of worshipping the Lord?

That is to say, when thy fingers grasp the paintbrush, it is as if thou wert at prayer in the Temple.

—'Abdu'l-Bahá

§§

BRIEFLY, ALL EFFORT and exertion put forth by man from the fullness of his heart is worship, if it is prompted by the highest motives and the will to do service to humanity.

This is worship: to serve mankind and to minister to the needs of the people.

Service is prayer.

—'Abdu'l-Bahá

Tablets and Meditations

*Intone, O My servant,
the verses of God that have been received by thee,
as intoned by them who have drawn nigh unto Him,
that the sweetness of thy melody
may kindle thine own soul,
and attract the hearts of all men.
Whoso reciteth, in the privacy of his chamber,
the verses revealed by God,
the scattering angels of the Almighty
shall scatter abroad
the fragrance of the words
uttered by his mouth,
and shall cause the heart
of every righteous man to throb.
Though he may, at first, remain unaware of its effect,
yet the virtue of the grace vouchsafed unto him
must needs sooner or later
exercise its influence upon his soul.
Thus have the mysteries
of the Revelation of God been decreed
by virtue of the Will of Him
Who is the Source of power and wisdom.*

—Bahá'u'lláh

TABLET OF AḤMAD

> "... the Tablet of Aḥmad, [has] been invested by Bahá'u'lláh with a special potency and significance, and should therefore be accepted as such and be recited by the believers with unquestioning faith and confidence, that through [it] they may enter into a much closer communion with God, and identify themselves more fully with His laws and precepts."
> —From a letter written on behalf of Shoghi Effendi

HE IS THE KING, the All-Knowing, the Wise! Lo, the Nightingale of Paradise singeth upon the twigs of the Tree of Eternity, with holy and sweet melodies, proclaiming to the sincere ones the glad tidings of the nearness of God, calling the believers in the Divine Unity to the court of the Presence of the Generous One, informing the severed ones of the message which hath been revealed by God, the King, the Glorious, the Peerless, guiding the lovers to the seat of sanctity and to this resplendent Beauty.

Verily this is that Most Great Beauty, foretold in the Books of the Messengers, through Whom truth shall be distinguished from error and the wisdom of every command shall be tested. Verily He is the Tree of Life that bringeth forth the fruits of God, the Exalted, the Powerful, the Great.

O Aḥmad! Bear thou witness that verily He is God and there is no God but Him, the King, the Protector, the Incomparable, the Omnipotent. And that the One Whom He hath sent forth by the name of 'Alí* was the true One from God, to Whose commands we are all conforming.

Say: O people be obedient to the ordi-

---

*The Báb.

nances of God, which have been enjoined in the Bayán by the Glorious, the Wise One. Verily He is the King of the Messengers and His book is the Mother Book did ye but know.

Thus doth the Nightingale utter His call unto you from this prison. He hath but to deliver this clear message. Whosoever desireth, let him turn aside from this counsel and whosoever desireth let him choose the path to his Lord.

O people, if ye deny these verses, by what proof have ye believed in God? Produce it, O assemblage of false ones.

Nay, by the One in Whose hand is my soul, they are not, and never shall be able to do this, even should they combine to assist one another.

O Aḥmad! Forget not My bounties while I am absent. Remember My days during thy days, and My distress and banishment in this remote prison. And be thou so steadfast in My love that thy heart shall not waver, even if the swords of the enemies rain blows upon thee and all the heavens and the earth arise against thee.

Be thou as a flame of fire to My enemies

and a river of life eternal to My loved ones, and be not of those who doubt.

And if thou art overtaken by affliction in My path, or degradation for My sake, be not thou troubled thereby.

Rely upon God, thy God and the Lord of thy fathers. For the people are wandering in the paths of delusion, bereft of discernment to see God with their own eyes, or hear His Melody with their own ears. Thus have We found them, as thou also dost witness.

Thus have their superstitions become veils between them and their own hearts and kept them from the path of God, the Exalted, the Great.

Be thou assured in thyself that verily, he who turns away from this Beauty hath also turned away from the Messengers of the past and showeth pride towards God from all eternity to all eternity.

Learn well this Tablet, O Aḥmad. Chant it during thy days and withhold not thyself therefrom. For verily, God hath ordained for the one who chants it, the reward of a hundred martyrs and a service in both worlds. These favors have We bestowed upon thee as a bounty on Our part and a mercy from Our presence, that thou mayest be of those who are grateful.

By God! Should one who is in affliction or grief read this Tablet with absolute sincerity, God will dispel his sadness, solve his difficulties and remove his afflictions.

Verily, He is the Merciful, the Compassionate. Praise be to God, the Lord of all the worlds.

—*Bahá'u'lláh*

Tablet on Purity

> . . . *in every aspect of life, purity and holiness, cleanliness and refinement, exalt the human condition . . .*
> —'Abdu'l-Bahá

O Friends of the Pure and Omnipotent God! To be pure and holy in all things is an attribute of the consecrated soul and a necessary characteristic of the unenslaved mind. The best of perfections is immaculacy and the freeing of oneself from every defect. Once the individual is, in every respect, cleansed and purified, then will he become a focal center reflecting the Manifest Light.

First in a human being's way of life must be purity, then freshness, cleanliness, and independence of spirit. First must the streambed be cleansed, then may the sweet river waters be led into it. Chaste eyes enjoy the beatific vision of the Lord and know what this encounter meaneth; a pure sense inhaleth the fragrances that blow from the rose gardens of His grace; a burnished heart will mirror forth the comely face of truth.

This is why, in Holy Scriptures, the counsels of heaven are likened to water, even as the Qur'an saith: "And pure water send We down from Heaven,"* and the Gospel: "Except a man be baptized of water and of the spirit, he cannot enter into the Kingdom of God."** Thus is it clear that the Teachings which come from God are heavenly outpourings of grace; they are rain-showers of divine mercy, and they cleanse the human heart.

My meaning is this, that in every aspect of life, purity and holiness, cleanliness and refinement, exalt the human condition and further

---

*Qur'an 25:50.
**Cf. John 3:5.

the development of man's inner reality. Even in the physical realm, cleanliness will conduce to spirituality, as the Holy Writings clearly state. And although bodily cleanliness is a physical thing, it hath, nevertheless, a powerful influence on the life of the spirit. It is even as a voice wondrously sweet, or a melody played: although sounds are but vibrations in the air which affect the ear's auditory nerve, and these vibrations are but chance phenomena carried along through the air, even so, see how they move the heart. A wondrous melody is wings for the spirit, and maketh the soul to tremble for joy. The purport is that physical cleanliness doth also exert its effect upon the human soul.

Observe how pleasing is cleanliness in the sight of God, and how specifically it is emphasized in the Holy Books of the Prophets; for the Scriptures forbid the eating or the use of any unclean thing. Some of these prohibitions were absolute, and binding upon all, and whoso transgressed the given law was abhorred of God and anathematized by the believers. Such, for example, were things categorically forbidden, the perpetration of which was accounted a most grievous sin, among them actions so loathsome that it is shameful even to speak their name.

But there are other forbidden things which do not cause immediate harm, and the injurious effects of which are only gradually produced: such acts are also repugnant to the Lord, and blameworthy in His sight, and repellent. The absolute unlawfulness of these, however, hath not been expressly set forth in the Text, but their avoidance is necessary to purity, cleanliness, the preservation of health, and freedom from addiction.

Among these latter is smoking tobacco, which is dirty, smelly, offensive—an evil habit, and one the harmfulness of which gradually becometh apparent to all. Every qualified physician hath ruled—and this hath also been proven by tests—that one of the components of tobacco is a deadly poison, and that the smoker is vulnerable to many and various diseases. This is why smoking hath been plainly set forth as repugnant from the standpoint of hygiene.

The Báb, at the outset of His mission, explicitly prohibited tobacco, and the friends one and all abandoned its use. But since those were times when dissimulation was permitted, and every individual who abstained from smoking was exposed to harassment, abuse and even death—the friends, in order not to advertise their beliefs, would smoke. Later on, the Book of Aqdas was revealed, and since smoking tobacco was not specifically forbidden there, the believers did not give it up. The Blessed Beauty, however, always expressed repugnance for it, and although, in the early days, there were reasons why He would smoke a little tobacco, in time He completely renounced it, and those sanctified souls who followed Him in all things also abandoned its use.

My meaning is that in the sight of God, smoking tobacco is deprecated, abhorrent, filthy in the extreme; and, albeit by degrees, highly injurious to health. It is also a waste of money and time, and maketh the user a prey to a noxious addiction. To those who stand firm in the Covenant, this habit is therefore censured both by reason and experience, and renouncing it will bring relief and peace of mind to all men. Furthermore, this will make it possible to have a fresh mouth and unstained fingers, and hair that is free of a foul and repellent smell. On receipt of this missive, the friends will surely, by whatever means and even over a period of time, forsake this pernicious habit. Such is my hope.

As to opium, it is foul and accursed. God protect us from the punishment He inflicteth on the user. According to the explicit Text of the Most Holy Book, it is forbidden, and its use is utterly condemned. Reason showeth that smoking opium is a kind of insanity, and experience attesteth that the user is completely cut off from the human kingdom. May God protect all against the perpetration of an act so hideous as this, an act which layeth in ruins the very foundation of what it is to be human, and which causeth the user to be dispossessed for ever and ever. For opium fasteneth on the soul, so that the user's conscience dieth, his mind is blotted away, his perceptions are eroded. It turneth the living into the dead. It quencheth the natural heat. No greater harm can be conceived than that which opium inflicteth. Fortunate are they who never even speak the name of it; then think how wretched is the user.

O ye lovers of God! In this, the cycle of Almighty God, violence and force, constraint and oppression, are one and all condemned. It is, however, mandatory that the use of opium be prevented by any means whatsoever, that perchance the human race may be delivered from this most powerful of plagues. And otherwise, woe and misery to whoso falleth short of his duty to his Lord.*

O Divine Providence! Bestow Thou in all things purity and cleanliness upon the people

---

*Cf. Qur'an 39:57.

of Bahá. Grant that they be freed from all defilement, and released from all addictions. Save them from committing any repugnant act, unbind them from the chains of every evil habit, that they may live pure and free, wholesome and cleanly, worthy to serve at Thy Sacred Threshold and fit to be related to their Lord. Deliver them from intoxicating drinks and tobacco, save them, rescue them, from this opium that bringeth on madness, suffer them to enjoy the sweet savors of holiness, that they may drink deep of the mystic cup of heavenly love and know the rapture of being drawn ever closer unto the Realm of the All-Glorious. For it is even as Thou hast said: "All that thou hast in thy cellar will not appease the thirst of my love—bring me, O cup-bearer, of the wine of the spirit a cup full as the sea!"

O ye, God's loved ones! Experience hath shown how greatly the renouncing of smoking, of intoxicating drink, and of opium, conduceth to health and vigor, to the expansion and keenness of the mind and to bodily strength.

There is today a people* who strictly avoid tobacco, intoxicating liquor and opium. This people is far and away superior to the others, for strength and physical courage, for health, beauty and comeliness. A single one of their men can stand up to ten men of another tribe. This hath proved true of the entire people: that is, member for member, each individual of this community is in every respect superior to the individuals of other communities.

Make ye then a mighty effort, that the purity and sanctity which, above all else, are cherished by 'Abdu'l-Bahá, shall distinguish the people of Bahá; that in every kind of excellence the people of God shall surpass all other human beings; that both outwardly and inwardly they shall prove superior to the rest; that for purity, immaculacy, refinement, and the preservation of health, they shall be leaders in the vanguard of those who know. And that by their freedom

---

*The Sikhs of India.

from enslavement, their knowledge, their self-control, they shall be first among the pure, the free and the wise.

—*'Abdu'l-Bahá*

TABLET OF THE HAIR

How long wilt thou soar in the realms of desire? Wings have I bestowed upon thee, that thou mayest fly to the realms of mystic holiness and not the regions of satanic fancy. The comb, too, have I given thee that thou mayest dress My raven locks, and not lacerate My throat.
—Bahá'u'lláh

HE IS THE ALL-MIGHTY!

My hair is my Messenger. It is calling aloud at all times upon the branch of fire within the hallowed and luminous Garden of Paradise, that perchance the inmates of the realm of creation may detach themselves from the world of dust and ascend unto the retreats of nearness—

the Spot where the Fire seeketh illumination from the light of the countenance of God, the Glorious, the Powerful.

O ye that have consecrated yourselves to this Fire! Sing ye melodies, pour out sweet tones, rejoice with exceeding gladness and make haste to attain the presence of Him Who is the Object of adoration, bearing witness that no God is there besides God, the All-Knowing, the All-Wise, the All-Compelling.

He is the God of Wisdom!

My hair is My Phoenix. Therefore hath it set itself upon the blazing fire of My Face and receiveth sustenance from the garden of My Countenance. This is the station wherein the Son of "Imrán"* removed from the feet of selfish desire the coverings of the attachment to all else but Him and was illumined by the splendors of the Light of holiness in the undying Fire kindled by God, the Potent, the Gracious, the Ever-Forgiving.

*Moses

He is the Most Excellent, the Best Beloved!

A lock of My hair is My Cord. He who layeth fast hold on it shall never to all eternity go astray, for therein is his guidance to the splendors of the Light of His beauty.

He is God!

My hair is My Veil whereby I conceal My beauty, that haply the eyes of the non-believers among My servants may not fall upon it. Thus do We conceal from the sight of the ungodly the glorious and sublime beauty of Our Countenance

He is the Eternal!

My hair beareth witness for My beauty that verily I am God and that there is none other God but me. In My ancient eternity I have ever been God, the One, the Peerless, the Everlasting, the Ever-living, the Ever-Abiding, the Self-Subsistent.

O denizens of the everlasting Realm! Let your ears be attentive to the stirrings of this restless and agitated hair, as it moveth upon the Sinai of Fire, within the precincts of Light, this celestial Seat of divine Revelation. Indeed there is no God besides me. In My most ancient pre-existence I have ever been the King, the Sovereign, the Incomparable, the Eternal, the Single, the Everlasting, the Most Exalted.

O peoples of the heavens and of the earth! Were ye to sanctify your ears ye would hear My hair proclaim that there is none other God except Him, and that He is One in His Essence and in everything that beareth relationship unto Him. And yet how fiercely have you caviled at this beauty; not withstanding that the outpourings of His grace have encompassed all that dwell in the billowing oceans of His Revelation and Creation. Be ye fair therefore in your judgment concerning His upright Religion, for the love of this Youth who is rid-ing high upon the snow-white She-Camel betwixt earth and heaven; and be ye firm and steadfast in the path of Truth.

—*Bahá'u'lláh*

THE MAID OF HEAVEN

Exalted be God, her creator. No eye hath ever seen any being like unto Her.
—Bahá'u'lláh

WHILE ENGULFED IN TRIBULATIONS I heard a most wondrous, a most sweet voice, calling above My head. Turning My face, I beheld a Maiden—the embodiment of the remembrance of the name of My Lord—suspended in the air before Me. So rejoiced was she in her very soul that her countenance shone with the ornament of the good-pleasure of God, and her cheeks glowed with the brightness of the All-Merciful. Betwixt earth and heaven she was raising a call which captivated the hearts and minds of men. She was imparting to both My inward and outer being tidings which rejoiced My soul, and the souls of God's honored servants.

Pointing with her finger unto My head, she addressed all who are in heaven and all who are on earth, saying: "By God! This is the Best-Beloved of the worlds, and yet ye comprehend not. This is the Beauty of God amongst you, and the power of His sovereignty within you, could ye but understand. This is the Mystery of God and His Treasure, the Cause of God and His glory unto all who are in the kingdoms of Revelation and of creation, if ye be of them that perceive."

—Bahá'u'lláh

§§

O SON OF JUSTICE! In the night-season the beauty of the immortal Being hath repaired from the emerald height of fidelity unto the

Sadratu'l-Muntahá,* and wept with such a weeping that the concourse on high and the dwellers of the realms above wailed at His lamenting.

Whereupon there was asked, Why the wailing and weeping?

He made reply: As bidden I waited expectant upon the hill of faithfulness, yet inhaled not from them that dwell on earth the fragrance of fidelity. Then summoned to return I beheld, and lo! certain doves of holiness were sore tried within the claws of the dogs of earth. Thereupon the Maid of heaven hastened forth unveiled and resplendent from Her mystic mansion, and asked of their names, and all were told but one. And when urged, the first letter thereof was uttered, whereupon the dwellers of the celestial chambers rushed forth out of their habitation of glory. And whilst the second letter was pronounced they fell down, one and all, upon the dust. At that moment a voice was heard from the inmost shrine: "Thus far and no farther."

*The Tree beyond which there is no passing; a symbol for the Manifestation of God.

Verily We bear witness to that which they have done and now are doing.
—Bahá'u'lláh

§§

Step out of Thy holy chamber, O Maid of Heaven, inmate of the Exalted Paradise! Drape thyself in whatever manner pleaseth Thee in the silken Vesture of Immortality, and put on, in the name of the All-Glorious, the broidered Robe of Light. Hear, then, the sweet, the wondrous accent of the Voice that cometh from the Throne of Thy Lord, the Inaccessible, the Most High.

Unveil Thy face, and manifest the beauty of the black-eyed Damsel, and suffer not the servants of God to be deprived of the light of Thy shining countenance. Grieve not if Thou hearest the sighs of the dwellers of the earth, or the voice of the lamentation of the denizens of heaven. Leave them to perish on the dust of extinction. Let them be reduced to nothingness, inasmuch as the flame of hatred hath been kindled within their breasts. Intone, then, before the face of the peoples of earth and heaven, and in a most melodious voice, the anthem of praise, for a remembrance of Him Who is the King of the names and attributes of God. Thus have We decreed Thy destiny. Well able are We to achieve Our purpose.

Beware that Thou divest not Thyself, Thou Who art the Essence of Purity, of Thy robe of effulgent glory. Nay, enrich Thyself increasingly, in the kingdom of creation, with the incorruptible vestures of Thy God, that the beauteous image of the Almighty may be reflected through Thee in all created things and the grace of Thy Lord be infused in the plenitude of its power into the entire creation.

If Thou smellest from any one the smell of the love of Thy Lord, offer up Thyself for him, for We have created Thee to this end, and have covenanted with Thee, from time immemorial, and in the presence of the congregation of Our well-favored ones, for this very purpose. Be not impatient if the blind in heart hurl down the shafts of their idle fancies upon Thee. Leave them to themselves, for they follow the promptings of the evil ones.

Cry out before the gaze of the dwellers of heaven and of earth: I am the Maid of Heaven, the Offspring begotten by the Spirit of Bahá. My habitation is the Mansion of His Name, the All-Glorious. Before the Concourse on high I was adorned with the ornament of His names. I was wrapt within the veil of an inviolable security, and lay hidden from the eyes of men. Methinks that I heard a Voice of divine and incomparable sweetness, proceeding from the right hand of the God of Mercy, and lo, the whole Paradise stirred and trembled before Me, in its longing to hear its accents, and gaze on the beauty of Him that uttered them. Thus have We revealed in this luminous Tablet, and in the sweetest of languages, the verses which the Tongue of Eternity was moved to utter in the Qayyumu'l-Asmá.*

—*Bahá'u'lláh*

---

*The Báb's major work, a commentary on the Surah of Joseph in the Qur'an, the first chapter of which was revealed on the evening of May 22, 1844.

THE TABLET OF THE VIRGIN*

I am the Maid of Heaven, the Offspring begotten by the Spirit of Bahá.
—Bahá'u'lláh

O MY NAMESAKE: Listen to My Call from around My Throne, so that it may summon thee to a Sea which has no boundary and to whose depths no diver has reached. Verily, thy Lord is knowing and generous. Verily, We desired to bestow Our Favor upon thee by mentioning that which We have seen, so that thou mayest behold a Luminous World in this dark world, and that thou mayest realize that We

---

*Lawh-i Ruyá, also known as The Tablet of the Vision.

have Worlds within this world, and offer thanks to thy Lord, the All-knowing.

Verily, if He wished He could make the rays of the sun manifest from an atom, and the waves of the sea from a drop. He hath power, as He hath set forth in detail: the knowledge of what was and what will be, out of a point.

Verily, We were seated on the Throne when a luminous Virgin clad in the finest white robe entered. She became like the full moon rising from the horizon of heaven.

Exalted be God, her creator. No eye hath ever seen any being like unto Her.

When she opened her mouth heaven and earth were illumined as though the Essence of Eternity reflected upon her its light.

Exalted be God, her creator. No eye hath ever seen any being like unto Her.

She smiled and bent like the stem of a reed in the presence of the Merciful One.

Exalted be He who made her manifest. No eye hath ever seen any being like unto Her.

Then she walked and moved about without any intention or will upon her part as if the needle of love were attracted by the magnet of the Beauty that shone in front of her.

Exalted be her creator. No eye hath ever seen any being like unto Her.

She walked while Glory was in attendance upon her and the Kingdom of Beauty was heralded in front of her, praising her matchless beauty, her winning ways and symmetry of form.

Exalted be her creator. No eye hath ever seen any being like unto Her.

Then We beheld jet-black hair hanging over her white throat, as though day and night embraced each other in this most glorious Station and highest Existence.

Exalted be her creator. No eye hath ever seen any being like unto Her.

When We observed her face, We found a point hidden under a veil, belonging to unity, shining forth from the horizon of her brow, as though through it the Tablets of the Love of the Merciful in the contingent world, and the volumes of the Lovers in all horizons, were fully explained.

Exalted be her creator. No eye hath ever seen any being like unto Her.

There was another point upon her breast which spoke of that point.

Exalted be the Lord of the Hidden and the Manifest who created her. No eye hath ever seen any being like unto Her.

The Temple of God arose and began to walk, and she walked behind, listening to, shaken and attracted by, the Verses of her Lord.

Blessed be He who created her. No eye hath ever seen any being like unto Her.

Then her joy, her delight and her enthusiasm increased to such a degree that she was changed and swooned. When she recovered her senses she drew near and said: "May my soul be a sacrifice to Thy imprisonment, O Secret of the unseen in the kingdom of creation!"

No eye hath ever seen any being like unto Her.

She remained looking at the dawning place of the Throne like one intoxicated and bewildered, until she placed her hand about the neck of her Lord and drew Him to her. As she drew nearer We took from her what was revealed in the treasured Red Epistle by My most exalted Pen.

Exalted be her creator. No eye hath ever seen any being like unto Her.

Then she bowed her head and rested her face upon her two fingers, as though a new moon had come into conjunction with a full moon.

Exalted be her creator. No eye hath ever seen any being like unto Her.

At this point she cried and said: "May the whole existence be a sacrifice to Thy afflictions, O King of heaven and earth! How long wilt Thou entrust Thyself to these people in the city of 'Akká? Go to Thy other Kingdoms, to the stations of that to which the eyes of the people of names have never turned!"

Whereupon We smiled.

Learn from this sweet narrative that which

We intend to describe of the hidden Secret which is manifest and yet most concealed, O people of wisdom among the companions of My Crimson Ark. This narrative coincides with the day which is the anniversary of the birth of My Herald,* who spoke eloquently of Me and of My Sovereignty, and informed the people of the heaven of My intention, the sea of My will, and the sun of My manifestation. We honored it with another day to which was manifested the Concealed Essence, the treasured Secret, and the preserved Mystery, the One through whom the inhabitants of the Kingdom of Names were shaken with bewilderment and those that are in heaven and earth are stunned, except those whom We secured with Our own authority and power. I am powerful in whatsoever I wish. There is no God but Me, the Knowing, the Wise.

Blessed is he who has inhaled from the fragrance of God in this day which is the dawning

---

*The Báb.

point of manifestation and the dayspring of My Name, the Forgiver, and in which the fragrance wafted, the spirit moved, the attraction raised up those who were in their graves, and Mount Sinai cried out: "The Kingdom belongeth to God, the Wise!" and in which every seeker obtained his desire, every man, knowing God, attained blessings, and every traveler in the way of God found the divine Right Path.

—Bahá'u'lláh

Editor's Note:

This book was compiled for use by men. However, it should be noted that all Bahá'í scriptures may be used by women, as well as by men. The use of masculine nouns and pronouns (e.g., he, him) in the text is an accident of language. English usage demands masculine forms, under certain circumstances, to represent both men and women. The phrase "a new race of men," for instance, is clearly intended to refer to all of humanity, not just to males. Similarly, other masculine forms should be understood to be universal in intent.

The singular pronoun in Persian is gender neutral. English has no equivalent to this, so the word must be translated as either "she" (when referring to a woman), or as "he" (for a man, or for both men and women). Plural pronouns (they, them) are gender neutral in both languages.

Gender in Arabic is more complicated, but presents similar problems for translation.